Classic
JAGUAR
WORLD

CAR
MECHANICS

JAGUAR
MONTHLY

JAGUAR XJS RESTORATION & MAINTENANCE

BY JIM PATTEN

Published by
KELSEY PUBLISHING LTD

Printed in Singapore by Stamford Press Pte Ltd.
On behalf of Kelsey Publishing Ltd,
Cudham Tithe Barn, Berry's Hill,
Cudham, Kent TN16 3AG
Tel: 01959 541444 Fax: 01959 541400

ISBN 1 873098 54 5

Acknowledgements
With additional features from *Jaguar Monthly* and *Car Mechanics,* Nigel Thorley and Leslie Thurston.

INTRODUCTION

The number of leading writers who have the knowledge and experience to write on the subject of Jaguars, are very few, as I soon discovered two years ago when I was pitched into editing a monthly Jaguar magazine. And of them, those with a serious technical and practical background are even fewer, perhaps no more than three or four. Jim Patten must be numbered high, if not first, in that very select band.

He is one the few Jaguar journalists who has actually got right down to it, getting his hands dirty restoring Jaguars. This attribute no doubt accounts for the insight he brings to Jaguar technical and practical coverage.

Surprisingly, to date there have been no practical books on the XJS, the longest-running and most popular Jaguar of all time. However, this book fills that gap in excellent fashion, with all Jim Patten's flair and talent for explaining techniques in an easy-to-follow style.

The core of this book is Jim Patten's extensive series of articles from *Jaguar World* magazine, covering the magazine's project car, a 1988 XJS 3.6 Coupe, and, Jim's 'Service & Survival Guide', from *Car Mechanics.* Supplemented by the 'XJS Buying & Fettling' guide from *Jaguar Monthly,* XJS Cabriolet and XJS Converible 'Star Buys' by Nigel Thorley, and finally a feature of XJS collectibles by Leslie Thurston.

At the same time any XJS owner or lover, even those who seldom lift a spanner, should find the series of features that come together in this book, a fascinating read.

Gordon Wright January 2001

CONTENTS

A bit more than a 'flesh wound': our XJS in post accident condition.

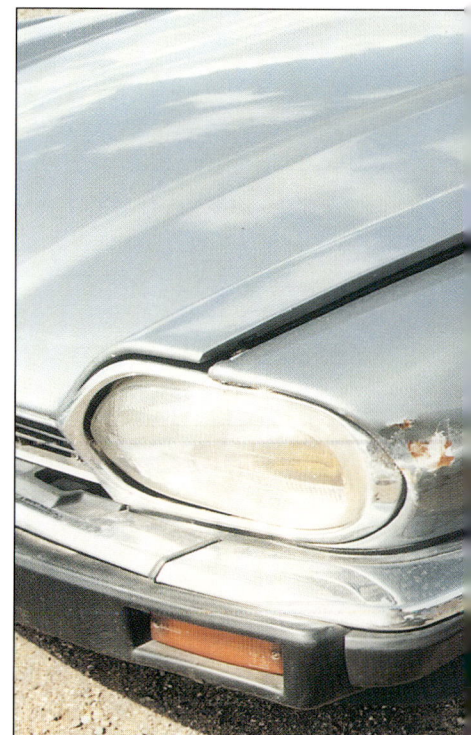

1 *It was the off-side that took the brunt of the impact but it would appear that only one chrome bumper blade is destroyed.*

2 *The near-side took a hit as well and the wing is too far gone to be saved. The wing movement caused a slight bend to the door. Derek 'dressed' this out with a panel beating hammer and dolly.*

3.6 XJ-S
Project Car

IN ASSOCIATION WITH
DAVID MANNERS

PART 1

What can you get for less than three grand? See what we came up with as Jim Patten kicks off our latest project.

"He's finally flipped you know. Bought a crashed XJ-S now. Barmy if you ask me. What's that? Oh, yes please, a pint of Ol' Wallop if you'd be so kind."

Yes, the bar talk is right. We've bought an accident damaged XJ-S. I know I should ignore the sceptics and just get right on with the job but unfortunately, suspicion surrounds accident-damaged cars. Shades of back streets, pop-rivets and two separate cars joined at the centre. I'm always slightly amused that repaired cars are about as welcome as a wooden leg while terminally rusty MGBs, Morris Minors and even XKs are thrown together in garden sheds to be declared 'restored classics'.

Think about it. I can chuck an 'E' type's original body away and replace it with one of unknown origins at home and as long as the car passes its MoT, I can use it. Yet a written-off accident damaged car is black listed and will not be removed from the list until a recognised repair has been effected and a thorough check over at an independent authorised centre has been carried out.

Let's get one thing clear from the start. A car is an accident damage write off not necessarily because of some life-threatening fault but almost invariably because it is deemed by the insurers or the owner to be beyond economic repair. Given the repair shops' hourly r

ate, the cost of new spares (all insurance repairs are based on new parts prices) and the resale value, it doesn't take long before the arithmetic takes over. Workshop time is expensive, especially if a body-jig is used. No car having suffered substantial body damage should escape a full alignment check. The slightest repair error could make for an extremely dangerous car and no matter how passionate we are about our hobby, it pales into insignificance when people's safety is at stake.

The mainstream accident repair industry is a very responsible body with many safeguards in place designed for the consumer's protection. Repairs must be done in such a way as to be indistinguishable from the manufacturer's result, even down to the type of welding – spot-welds, for example, must be of the same number and position as original. Afterwards, companies such as Autolign give the car a complete alignment check. That alone is expensive; it's usually related to the value of the car but reckon on £400-500.

Targets

Accident repairs are only one area of this project, however. Right from the start I

Continued

Continued

THE CAR:
XJS 3.6 coupe, manufactured 1988, VIN: SAJJNAEC3CA154441, purchased as a damaged write-off, December, 1997.

3.6 XJ-S Project Car

3 *Looking down on the off-side inner wing, it is evident that the impact stopped here with a small crease in the inner wing.*

accepted that it would not be an economical proposition, purely because of the extra jobs we want to incorporate into the series. How could we drop the front and rear axles without attending to the suspension, for instance? So we will be showing many jobs which are commonly faced by XJ-S owners, from replacing a rusty rear quarter panel, through suspension overhaul, to a simple headlamp unit change. Then, once the car is on the road, we'll be running it for a while and maybe doing one or two upgrades.

We are very pleased to welcome David Manners on board as our sponsor. David takes a keen interest in the XJ-S and is not frightened to make huge

4 *This shows the front suspension beam, bent at the front 'doughnut' mount. The cross-member beneath the radiator is just showing surface rust so we can save it now.*

5 *Beneath the car and the gearbox mount where it obviously caught a kerb and bent. One bolt has stripped out.*

6 *Derek Swinger has peeled back the top skin where it was rusting on the off-side inner wing. With the engine removed, we can carry out a permanent repair.*

investments in parts, even if no immediate cash return is evident. Enthusiasts should be grateful for his farsighted approach – when XJ-S parts vanish from official dealer's shelves, a quick call to the David Manners helpline should sort the problem out. We will also be able to check on the quality of the products his company stocks and, believe me, we tell it how it is. But Davids approves of that, and would have it no other way.

Our car

"Oh, what have you bought?" cried Derek Swinger of the Romford Bodyshop, "Why didn't you take me with you when you bought it?" I've learnt to accept these castigations from Derek now but I am so confident in his abilities as a body man to perform miracles and get me out of the smelly stuff that I can take it on the chin.

There was little point in buying a car that had a slight biff; better to go the whole way (so I told myself). Our XJ-S came through Alan Duke at XJ-S Spares. It's a 1988 model, plastered with main dealer (Grange Motors) stickers and appears to have been well cared for pre-accident. Damaged cars rarely come

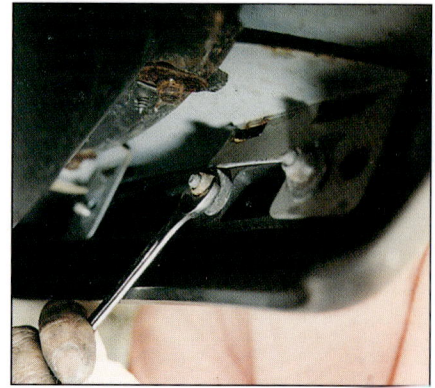

7 *Amazingly, all the nuts holding the bumper rubbers came undone. The main bumper section was removed from the buffer, although one had sheared in the accident.*

with service history so we may well have to carry out some detective work; I'm told that Grange at Brentwood keep all their old service data so we may be in luck.

Derek soon identified the problem areas on the car. The main impact was on the off-side which appears to have pushed the front of the car over slightly and moved one side up. The front suspension cross-member has also bent – apparently they are a weak spot and can even distort under severe 'kerbing'. The car obviously spun around, or at least went sideways, and mounted a kerb or other structure, as the rear axle cage is creased, the gearbox mount has been bent and one bolt has been pulled out.

Before buying the car I was able to hear it running and even drive it across the yard. The engine fan had been

8 *Although the front wings are bolted on, there is one weld at the very end of the lower quarter, just ahead of the front wheel.*

hitting the radiator but Alan Duke disconnected the fan belt and we were able to start the car. Everything seemed to be in perfect working order so we agreed a price and had the car delivered straight to the Romford Bodyshop.

We're off

We've drawn up a shopping list. The bonnet is okay although the hinges are bent, but we'll need a pair of front wings (second-hand), headlights, one bumper blade with rubber, a pair of lower

9 *See how this lower quarter has suffered in the crash. Derek Swinger removes the assembly in one and then takes it to the bench to retrieve the salvageable items.*

10 *This type of rust is typical XJ-S and will be present on virtually all cars of this age now unless they have been rust-proofed early in their lives.*

quarter sections and the bumper reinforcing bar. It seems the grille escaped damage. Our plan is to obtain the panels, straighten the car, rebuild the front and rear axles and then re-assemble. To do the job right, the engine and gearbox had to come out. In the time it took me to return home, make up a shopping list and load the Nikon, Derek had the XJ-S stripped and ready to go. "I've got Mr Skilleter's XK 150 to finish and I can't wait for you arty types," Derek declared.

It's a little different stripping a car that's been bent. Access is sometimes more difficult, but often easier, as panels which are going to be replaced anyway can be bent, cut, bashed or otherwise mutilated. The bonnet was the first to be removed, and this, with its struts, was taken away for safekeeping. Next, Derek removed all lights and remains of glass just to clear the sharp stuff. The bumper gave readily by being released from the two buffer extensions. Next came the

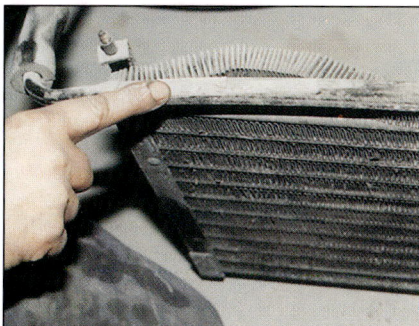

11 *Almost made it – these radiator fins have popped out of the frame, and there may even be a twist present.*

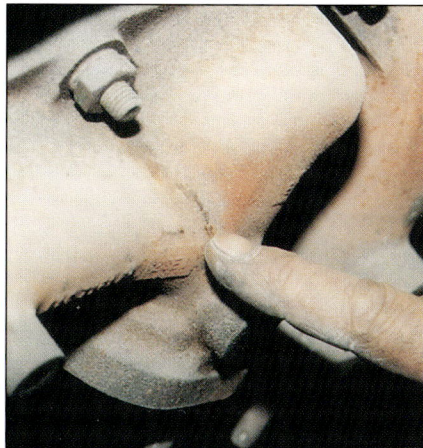

12 *Nothing to do with the accident, this crack in the manifold has been there for some time. We need a replacement.*

13 *We're lucky that the XJS is fairly rust-free. There is this bubbling plus some corrosion on the rear lower quarter.*

14 *Alan Duke at XJ-S Spares located a complete suspension beam from another 3.6 XJ-S. We will strip it down and use the best parts from this with the original beam, replacing all the perishables.*

grille, and then work began on the wings.

Bolts secure the wing along the engine bay lip, inside the inner wing to the bulkhead side, on top of the sill and a row along the lower quarter. Oddly enough, there is just one weld, and that's at the very end of the lower quarter, in front of the front wheel.

With the wings off, we spotted rust in the reinforcing strip along the inner wing. In fact, this was a golden opportunity to renew and preserve many normally unseen danger areas.

Externally, all that remained now were the lower quarters, lower grille and

15 *The bonnet hinge on the left is a second-hand replacement, that on the right is original. See how it has bent slightly.*

spoiler. All came off without a fight. The radiator had moved forward very slightly and, although the fins had popped out, it was still holding coolant. Derek drained all oils and water before removing the radiators (coolant and air conditioning).

Now we had our chance to have a good look around. The usual rust was present on the offside inner wing but, with the engine removed, we could carry out a permanent repair. Derek spotted a cracked exhaust manifold, but said that it had nothing to do with the accident. Our shopping list grew, as we added a hose set, engine drive belts, mounts and so on. Alan Duke located a front beam from a 3.6 XJ-S, so there's a

job for me to do in stripping that down.

The Skilleter XK 150 then took priority, as its wanted in time for XK 50 but we will return in the next issue when we straighten ourselves, and the car, out.

Acknowledgements.
Car supplied by: XJ-S Spares, Tel: 01992 768007
Transported by: Alpha Autos Tel: 0836 232114
Bodywork by: The Romford Bodyshop, 11 Maldon Road, Crow Lane, Romford, Essex RM7 0JB, Tel: 01708 723745

3.6XJ-S
PROJECT CAR

DAVID MANNERS LTD
THE CLASSIC SPECIALIST

THE CAR:
XJ-S 3.6 coupe manufactured 1988,
VIN: SAJJNAEC3CA15441,
purchased as damaged write-off December 1977.
Objective: repair, restore, run and upgrade

**THE STORY SO FAR: Part 1
(Vol 10 no 4) - assessment, and
removing bumpers, front wings ,
radiators etc**

Part 2: Getting straight
. Jim Patten does a jig as body repairs start.

*"**All we need is** a little tug here and a bit of a nudge there. It'll soon be straight - don't worry." Derek Swinger's words reassured my apprehensive ears. It all seemed a great idea at the time to buy and sraighten a damaged Jaguar but when I saw the accuracy to which the body dimensions must be returned, I became rather scared.*

Engine out

As Derek seems to be able to glide through this work with the greatest of ease, we left the engine removal to him. With a sliding overhead electric hoist,taking the strain, engine and gearbox come out as an assembly. The obvious appendages were removed first of course: engine bay tie bars, propshaft, exhaust system and any water hoses still connected to the bulk-head (the radiator and air-conditioning

1. Removing the 3.6 litre engine is not as daunting as it might seem given that the right tools are at hand. NEVER try this using minimal equipment as failure could be lethal!

condenser had already been removed). When the auxiliary cooling fan came to be removed, we found the motor seized so that's another fault to remedy.

One really infuriating part was the oil cooler. Now ours was undamaged but as occurs in virtually every instance, when the unions are undone the thread from the cooler strips. The cooler is now useless and Jaguar's price is an outrageous £250. Luckily, David Manners offer an after-market replacement somewhere in the region of £65. Now that's what I call a saving. Back to the plot. On cars that have been running, the fuel system needs to be de-pressurised (remove the fuel pump fuse and run engine until all fuel

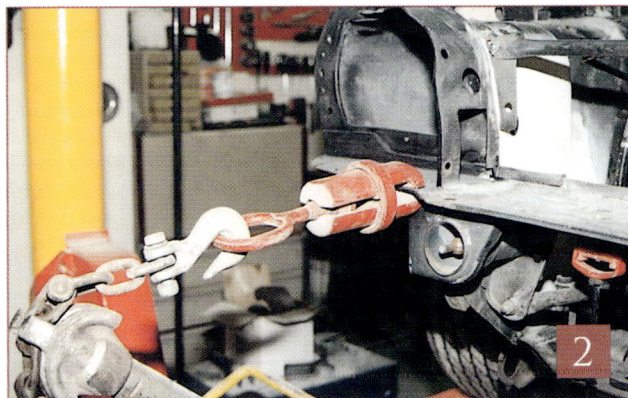

2. With various clamps mounted on the bodyshell, the Dataliner jig does its work in pulling the misshapen XJ-S back in line. The metal is pulled slightly over its point to allow 'spring-back'.

is used) before disconnecting the fuel pipes. Then the power steering pump is removed after the delivery/supply pipes are undone. Vacuum air pipes follow from servo, air conditioning and ECU. Finally all electrical

3. These markers are hung at strategic points over the bodyshell as clearly defined by the maker's instructions. A laser beam is fired through the gauge and when all measurements concur, then the shell is deemed straight.

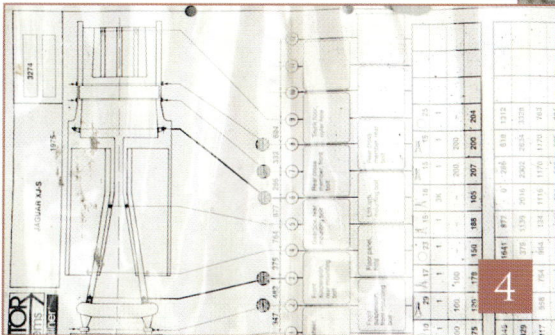

4. This diagram is used to position the marker gauges on the bodyshell and gives the precise measurements needed. If the repair is only slightly out, the laser will find out

5. Rust was found behind the front splash panel and although Derek cut out the effected area, he eventually decided to replace the whole panel, simply making another.

The straight and narrow

A Dataliner jig is a fancy piece of kit that secures a car on its rigid bed. From mounting points, lengths of chain pass over hydraulic rams to hook on to sturdy clamps. These clamps are fastened to strategic points on the body. Each car make and model has its own set of co-ordinates and Derek dug out those for the XJ-S. Suitably chained, connections are pulled apart. Working under the car, the speedo transducer is disconnected and the gearbox weight taken by a jack so that the gearbox mount can be taken off. If this sounds a bit too brief, most of the components mentioned can fit only one, blindingly obvious, way. Jaguar's own workshop manual also illustrates every part very clearly.

An engine sling was then fitted and the weight taken. Both engine mounts were removed and the engine was ready to lift. It came out at a pretty steep angle but with Derek's equipment it was a piece of cake. Once on the floor, the engine was put aside to be looked at later. No further surprises were found inside the bay.

the rams were pumped and the metal was gradually eased back to where the manufacturer intended it to be. Doing this by eye is not good enough. A series of markers are placed at precise points as dictated by the co-ordinates. The markers are transparent but bear various markers. Once they are positioned, a laser beam is attached to the jig. This fires off a perfectly straight beam of light that should pass through each marker at a specified point. Only when all markers accept this beam at a precise point can the car be considered straight. It was uncanny to see a thin red line pass directly through each marker at the exact spot. I was comforted. My magician had performed his trick and I was satisfied.

This sort of work is highly specialised and whilst competent enthusiasts may be capable of rust repairs and similar, it is absolutely vital that any structural re-alignment work be entrusted to professionals. Derek Swinger's bodyshop is recognised by the VBRA (Vehicle Body Repair Association) as an approved repairer so use a company similarly approved.

Cutting the rust

Now Derek could deal with the minor problem areas. Behind the splash panel on the off-side wing sits an overflow tank - an apt name as it overflows itself and deposits water on the metal base. Yes, you have it, rust swoops in and soon there is no panel for the tank to sit on. A straightforward enough shape that Derek was able to fabricate while I drank tea. We'll modify the overflow to take the water away in future.

6. The 3M Clean'n Strip wheel is perfect for surface rust like this. A couple of minutes had this small area back to shiny metal, ready for primer.

7. Derek offers up the new inner wing top rail to find out exactly what was needed. Instead of using the entire panel, he let-in the centre section only.

We had ordered new inner wing top rails from David Manners but as the end sections were so good, decided to use the centre section only. Each spot weld was taken out and the rusted section cut away. Then, by placing the new section alongside to determine where to cut, scribe marks were made and the rails cut to size. The new rails were

8. The rusted section of inner wing top rail is now being removed by first drilling out the necessary spot-welds. These can be found by rubbing the metal with a piece of coarse sanding paper.

used to cut steel sheet to the same size. Finally, this is welded into place using a continuous MiG weld. I've had various ideas about protecting this vulnerable area. Unfortunately one came a bit too late but I'll tell you anyway. A hole is drilled in the new repair section, near to the top edge. Once the metal has been welded in place, rust protector can be sprayed in between the two plates using a very thin nozzle as on an aerosol. There will be just sufficient gap to get the fluid to penetrate the sandwich. I may even take a chance with drilling a small hole even now. Other areas around the bulkhead allow rust to

9. This is what the inner wing looks like with the rail section removed. See how sound this is. The rustproofing nozzle will get easy access through those two holes conveniently located in the inner wing.

MiG welded to the old section but spot-welded along the top exactly as Jaguar intended. The whole of the inner box will be rustproofed later although the outside was treated with Waxoyl underseal.

There's absolutely no escape. Virtually every XJ-S more than three or four years old could have some rust in the engine bay inner wing. It's awkward to get at

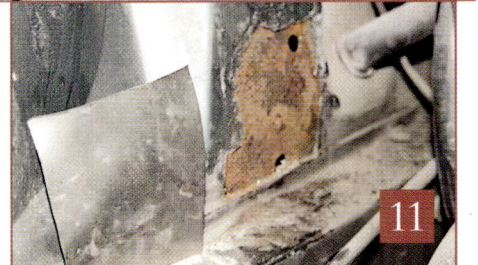

The completed job. Fresh metal has made for a perfect invisible repair. A coating of Waxoyl undersealant will help protect but of course, we will carry out thorough rustproofing later.
And inset:
If you doubt me, go look at your own car and you'll probably find rust here - directly below the shock-absorber mount. Derek has already trimmed back part of the metal and will make a repair section from the piece alongside.

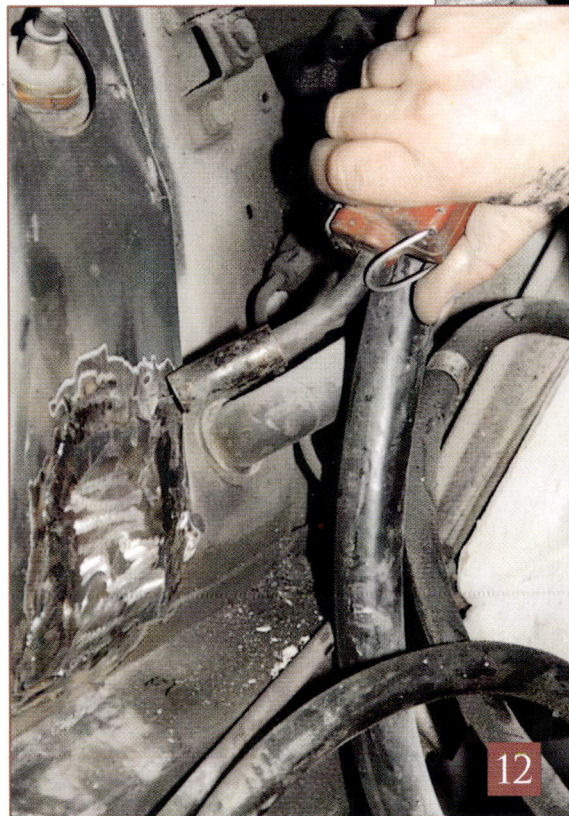

with the power unit installed but with engine out, repairs are easier. The metal is double skinned so great care is needed. Derek took the top skin back to where the rust finished and carefully used a cutting wheel on an angle grinder to get through the top skin. He didn't make a complete cut through but left a tiny piece behind and then worked the old metal out rather than risk cutting into the bottom layer.

We were still faced with surface rust on the remaining layer . 3M's Clean'n Strip wheel is perfect for this job, far better than any wire brush. Used on an electric drill, it seems to get into every tiny little crevice to leave the metal clean and shiny.

Only with all surface rust gone can repairs start. A cardboard template is cut until it fits perfectly into the affected area., then

get its foot in the door. These were soon dealt with using the 3M Clean'n Strip wheel and then protected with Comma Stop Rust - we reckon one of the best anti-rust primers on the market.

12. MiG welding completes the job that will be ground flush afterwards. With the engine removed, the inner wings will be repainted for a perfect job.

13. Undamaged but rusty nonetheless, this front panel will have to be replaced. Still obtainable from Jaguar at £69.50 - get yours while you can.

14. We were lucky to get a good second-hand front lower quarter panel to replace our crumpled one These parts are becoming increasingly rare.

Oh, for a wing

With Derek sorting out alignments, I was sent shopping for a couple of good second-hand wings and lower quarter panels. A decent lower panel would be good too. The easiest route would have been to order up a couple of new panels from David Manners and be done with it, but although I didn't intend to skimp on quality, there are limits and good used parts should always be considered where safety is not compromised . Eventually I tracked down a couple of wings and lower quarters (as well as the bonnet hinge) from Paul Banham. They had been removed from a car he recently

16. It's called initiative. Derek Swinger utilised a section of damaged door to repair the lower wing. The fully seam welded joints arecovered with sealer to keep out the damp. We'll double the protection by rustproofing later.

converted to 'wide body'. The whole lot came to £200 and although there was a small repair needed to one wing, it represented a huge saving over new.

Of course Derek complained but then he would. But I was impressed at how he tackled the job of repairing rust damage to the wing where it met the sill. On the reverse is a built in bracket that is used to fasten the wing to the sill top. Derek studied the shape for a while and then disappeared. He returned carrying a damaged door from a previous job. It turned out that the shape of the bottom of the skin, the return edge and the bottom of the doorshell, matched the XJ-S wing exactly. Indeed, when he cut the section out of the door and held it against

the wing, astonishingly, it looked like a manufacture's repair section. I'm sure Derek was pleased because he stopped nagging and made a cuppa to celebrate.

Next time I saw that wing, all rust had been cut out, the new section let in and it was indistinguishable from new. With the back cleaned off, primed with Comma Rust Stop, it was then sprayed with Waxoyl under-sealant.

Both lower quarter section were also cleaned up and found to be in top condition. Alas, I failed to locate a new front panel so we bought new. Luckily they are still available but it is a vulnerable part and it's only a question of time before they disappear from Jaguar's parts list But when that happens, I'm sure David Manners will

15. Good second-hand wings are hard to find so we were happy to have only this small amount of rust to deal with. The rest of the wing is perfect.

be there ready with a good replacement.

I guess you want to know how we got on with fitting the wings? Well, I can't tell you because I've run out of pages so that will have to wait until the next episode.

17. The back of the wing is fully covered with Waxoyl underseal ant for added protection. Again, once the car is finished, we will give it a full going over.

NEXT ISSUE
Body Beautiful

CAR SUPPLIED BY: XJ-S SPARES, TEL: 01992 768007
SPONSOR AND MAJOR PARTS SUPPLIER:
DAVID MANNERS LTD, TEL: 0121 544 4040
BODY AND PAINTWORK BY: THE ROMFORD BODYSHOP,
11 MALDON ROAD, ROMFORD, ESSEX RM7 OJB, TEL: 01708 723745

XJ-S

PROJECT CAR

In association with

DAVID MANNERS LTD
THE CLASSIC SPECIALIST

Part 3: Panelling up. Jim Patten attends the make over.

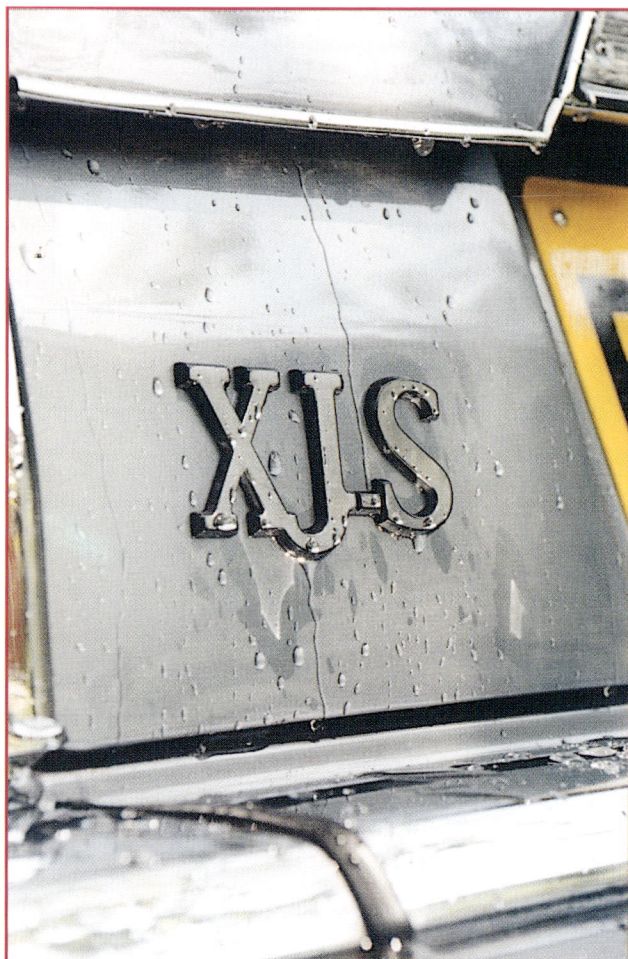

Now that the car is going straight, Derek Swinger at the Romford Bodyshop could concentrate on cosmetic items like front wings and bonnet. We had been lucky enough to source some excellent used front wings but there are still a few damaged or rusted parts to replace. Both headlight chrome surrounds were broken along with an indicator, a front bumper retaining bolt had sheared in the accident and one bumper blade was seriously twisted. So, with text and pictures, let's get on with it.

THE CAR:
XJ-S 3.6 coupe manufactured 1988,
VIN: SAJJNAEC3CA15441,
purchased as damaged write-off December 1997.
Objective: repair, restore, run and upgrade

THE STORY SO FAR: Part 1 (Vol 10 no 4) - assessment, and removing bumpers, front wings , radiators etc. Part 2 (Vol 10 no 5) - engine removal, body jigging, body repairs including inner and outer front wings and front panel.

Fit up

Part of the straightening procedure involved fitting the wings and bonnet to check alignments; during which Derek discovered that the bonnet was slightly kinked and would need straightening.

But before any panels were fitted, any suspect areas of surface rust were cleaned down using a 3M Clean 'n Strip wheel before being painted with Comma Rust Stop, an excellent rust preventing primer. Waxoyl undersealant covered the primer.

Each wing was fitted and aligned by moving it about courtesy of the slotted bolt holes. The bonnet was aligned at the top edge and each side edge. This showed that the off-side front edge needed

attention. Using a variety of skills which included wielding various levers and hammers, Derek was able to bring the bonnet

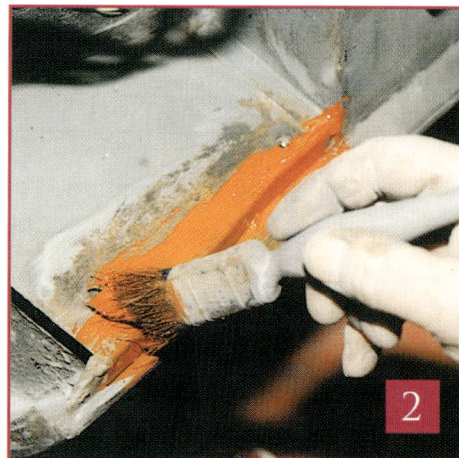

2. Any evidence of surface rust is cleaned away and treated with Comma Rust Stop.

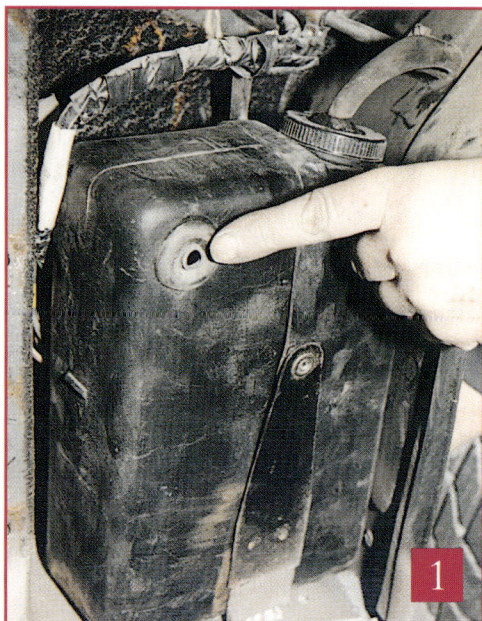

1. Overflow from the atmospheric recovery bottle drains on to the top of the sill and eventually causes the panel to rot.

3. Bonnet hinges are fitted, secured with 13mm bolts. Holes are slotted to allow for adjustment.

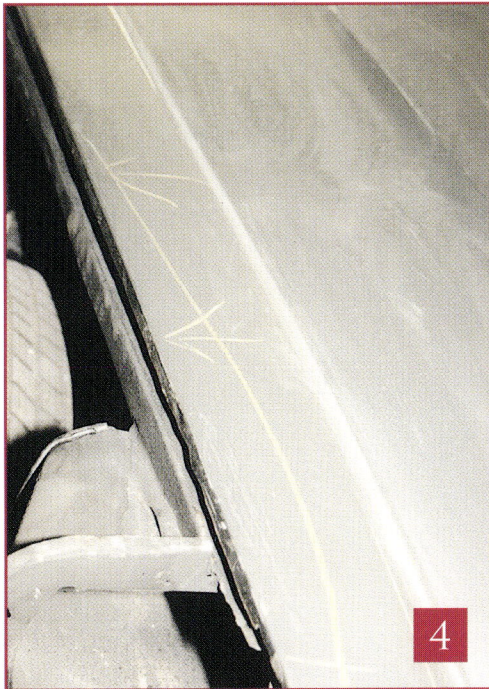

4. This is how Derek identifies an area needing attention. The bonnet edge had lifted, requiring it to be returned to its correct position, achieved with levers, hammers and a dolly.

getting in and provoking rust.

A bracket is fitted between the wing and the bulkhead to hold the long upright section in place. Alignment had to be arranged all over again as there is no real reference point.

This time, it was more difficult due to the sticky panel sealer. Attention had to be paid to door/wing gaps too, with both adjusted to get even and constant clearances.

edge down to meet the wing. When at last he was happy, all three panels could be bolted up tightly.

Panel Fit was laid between inner and outer wings - this is sealer strip on a roll and is positioned along the edge where the wing is bolted. As the bolts are tightened, so the sealer compresses and seals, preventing water

The bumper retaining bolt was a simple swap after getting a new replacement from David Manners. Our quarter panels were in pretty good order, just needing a good clean up. New nuts and bolts along with the oval type washers and they were fitted. That small weld was made at the end of the quarter where it fits to the wing and then ground back to make clean. Last of all, the aluminium inner wing splash panels were re-fitted using quality seam sealer from 3M to make the seal absolute, preventing water ingress and the two dissimilar metals touching.

never!" yelled Derek (or words to that effect), "it fits!"

One alteration was needed - the drain tube had to be cut from the old quarter and welded into the new. Quite simple except that the tube had to be in the right place so that it

Accept no quarter

"If that's repro, you can take it back where you found it - it's no good to me." Derek's words rung in the air. I explained that I was sure the new rear quarter panel was very good and came from our sponsor David Manners and we really ought to be nice to him. Well, he agreed to have a go but not before making it clear that if it didn't fit, he would put the cutting torch through it, like some panels he had seen from other so-called specialists. I watched while he got on with the job, cutting the bulk of the old panel away and then ground back around the welds, clearing the field for the new panel. I was nervous as he offered the Manners panel in place. "Well, I

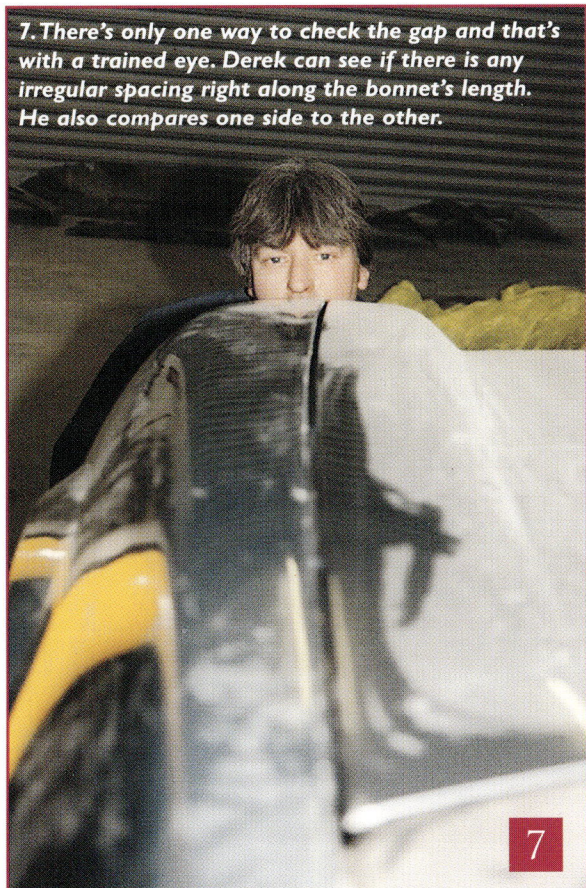

7. There's only one way to check the gap and that's with a trained eye. Derek can see if there is any irregular spacing right along the bonnet's length. He also compares one side to the other.

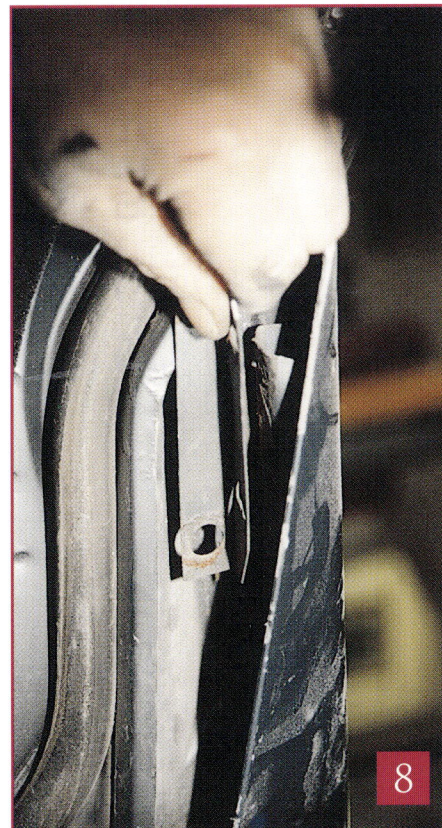

8. This bracket fits between the wing and the bulkhead. First on the wing and then to the car.

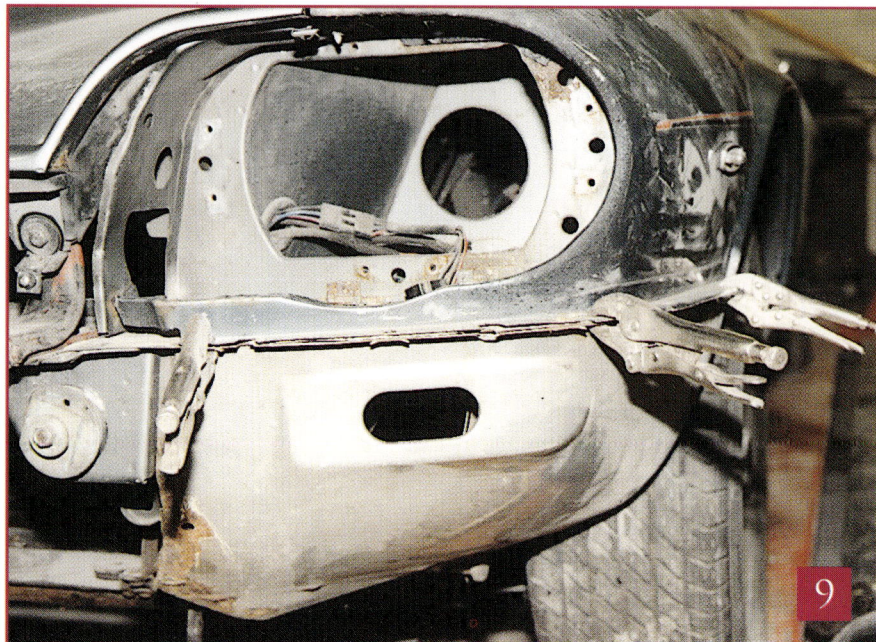

9. The second-hand front quarter panel is trial fitted before preparing it. Any adjustments or trimming can be done at this stage. None of which was necessary as it fitted okay.

10. Finally, the bonnet struts are bolted in place. These lose their efficiency over the years and become a regular item to replace. Ours were fine however.

11. Derek cuts the old rear quarter panel away, removing the 'loose' metal before getting to grips with the spot welds.

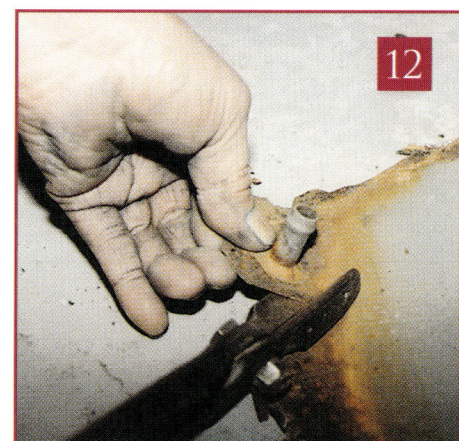

12. The drain tube is cut from the old quarter. See how the edge has rusted through lack of rust treatment. We will ensure that our new panel is protected.

didn't foul on anything and could be reached by the drain tube. It was clamped in place with grips, the spot welder taking care of the top section and the MiG finishing it off. No fettling, no trimming, the panel just fitted. What a relief. Thanks David!

A few spots of rust were spotted on the number plate light plinth. Derek prodded away and found a gaping hole. Not only that, it had been repaired in the past as some braze was unearthed. But as the only rust repair we have found on the entire car, it wasn't bad!

Before Derek started on the quarter, he did strip the rear lights and electric aerial out. Fairly straightforward stuff. The inner panels are removed from the boot to get access to

13. "I don't believe it, this panel actually fits." Derek is amazed that a 'pattern' replacement panel could really be correct!

14. Clamps hold the panel in place while a spot-welder completes the job.

16. A new bumper retaining bolt was obtained from David Manners. Replacement was a simple nut and bolt job.

15. Fully fitted, the new rear quarter panel is indistinguishable from new. Something about proof being in the pudding.

to carry out the paintwork. Time is a funny old thing. In this issue, you can read about our XK 150 and XJ-S. The XK 150 was actually painted before the XJ-S but the way the reports fall, both will appear to be in the bodyshop at the same time. But it's all an illusion, folks...

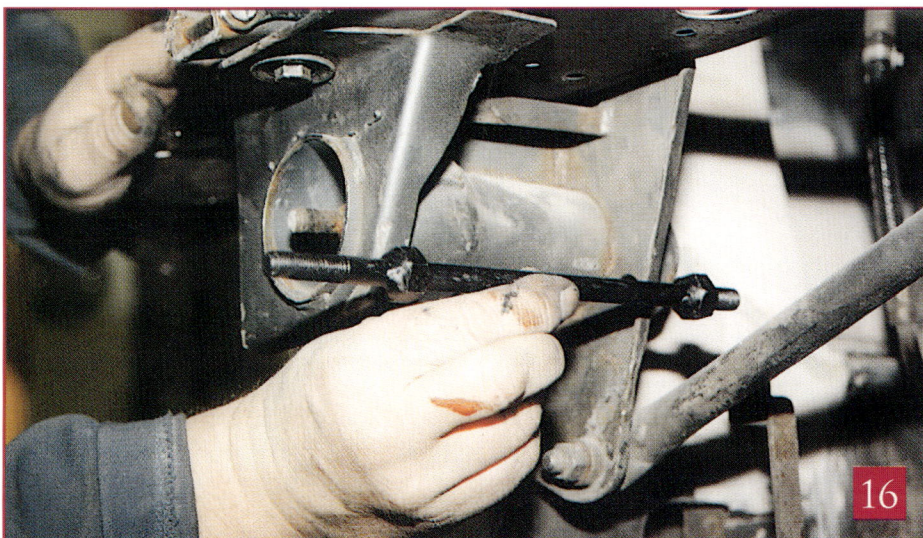

16.

ACKNOWLEDGEMENTS:
BODYWORK BY:
THE ROMFORD BODYSHOP,
11 MALDON ROAD,
CROW LANE, ROMFORD,
ESSEX RM7 0JB.
TEL: 01708 723745.

PARTS FROM:
DAVID MANNERS,
991 WOLVERHAMPTON ROAD,
OLDBURY, WEST MIDLANDS
B69 4RJ, TEL: 0121 544 4040,
FAX: 544 5558.

removing the passenger seat and getting inside the retaining section. Derek opened up the area, replaced the captive nut and closed up again. Then he could replace the carpet and seat.

At last our Jaguar was sitting all square wearing all of its panels. Over to Derek again

18. The only rust we found on the car that had been previously dealt with. A small hole soon grew and revealed a hidden brazed repair.

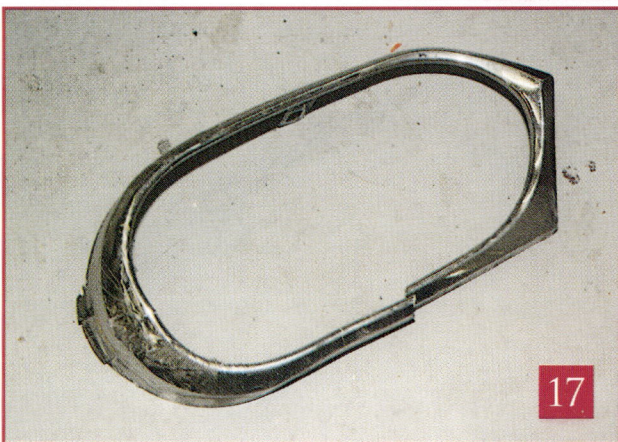

17.

17. Both light surrounds had suffered in the crash. Second-hand replacements were not to be found but David Manners did supply new.

the lights and connections. Retaining nuts are removed and lights extracted. The aerial followed as per the workshop manual which gave a good account of how to do the job.

Derek was on the ball remembering the gearbox support member. It had been bent awkwardly during the accident and looked as though a bolt had pulled through. It had and the captive was missing. This involved

18.

19

XJ-S PROJECT CAR

In association with
DAVID MANNERS LTD
THE CLASSIC SPECIALIST

Part 4: A Twist in the Tail. Jim Patten finds that the rear axle cage has also been damaged, and we follow the rear suspension overhaul.

1 An acrobatic-looking Alan Slawson receives the rear suspension unit prior to its stripping down.

THE CAR:
XJ-S 3.6 coupe manufactured 1988,
VIN: SAJJNAEC3CA15441,
purchased as damaged write-off
December 1997.
Objective: repair, restore, run and upgrade

THE STORY SO FAR:
Part 1 (Vol 10 no 4) - assessment, and removing bumpers, front wings , radiators etc.
Part 2 (Vol 10 no 5) - engine removal, body jigging, body repairs including inner and outer front wings and front panel.
Part 3 (Vol 10 no 6) - body repairs including fitting wings and rear quarter panel, inner wing repairs etc.

You can't help but pity Derek Swinger at the Romford Bodyshop. Both Jaguar World project cars in his workshop at once. So we thought we would give him a break this month and look at the rear axle on the XJ-S.

We always knew that something was amiss at the back of our car - the angle one of the wheels was at, who wouldn't?

It appears that the shunt had pushed the frame against the mountings and these had bent with the force. There was also a crease on the frame itself so we would need a replacement frame at least along with some of the components as well. Paul Banham

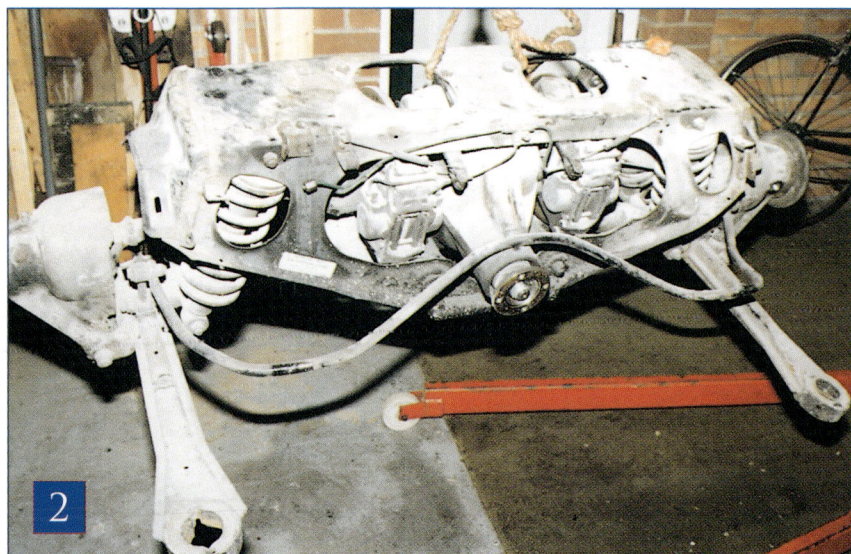

2 As removed from the car: the complete IRS is ready to be taken apart. It's white because of fall-out from Derek's flatting operations in his paintshop.

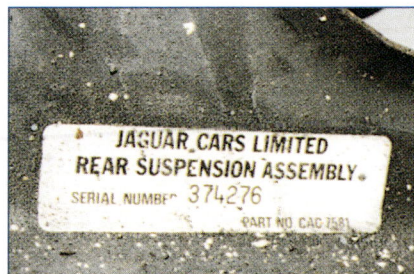

JAGUAR CARS LIMITED
REAR SUSPENSION ASSEMBLY.
SERIAL NUMBER 374276
PART NO CAC 7581

3 All later cars had this identity number on the axle cage.

4 Work begins as the bottom pan is undone to give access to the wishbones and diff.

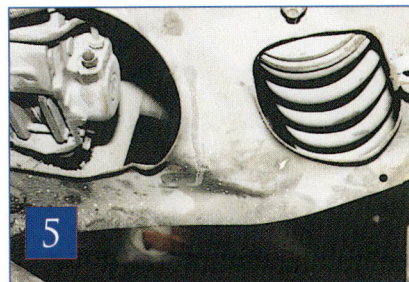

5 See how the frame has buckled in the region between the damper and differential.

6 This rubber bush has become detached from the metal sleeve so that metal now turns on metal without the resilience of rubber.

7 Note the spacer washer between the lower wishbone and the shock absorber. The shaft taps through and is completely removable.

8 The bolt securing the radius arm to the wishbone is cut half across the head to enable it to clear the shock absorber tube.

9 When the fulcrum shaft was dismantled, it was found that this grease seal had been split for some time. Grease would soon have vacated the area.

had a spare rear suspension unit with everything but the diff. After a bit of negotiating, flattery and arm wrestling, it was ours. But it pays to check. After close examination following shot blasting, we found a crease in this one too plus a small split around one of the bolt holes. Paul was very good about it and we came to an arrangement where we kept the bits but returned the frame. Our old chum, Dick Bradley, came up with a good alternative and we were finally in business.

Alan Slawson, rear suspension builder par excellence, was drafted in to do the complete job. We were not looking for a total rebuild as our unit was fundamentally sound, so the brief was to replace what was needed. If you are looking for a detailed blow by blow account, then you could do no better than order the Jaguar World XK Engine book which despite its title has a thorough account of the Jaguar IRS rebuild. But the first job was to remove the unit from the car.

Get back down

The exhaust system runs through the axle cage and as this was to be replaced anyway (it too was damaged), it could just be cut away. I'm afraid to admit that initially I tried to do the job properly and undo all of the nuts and bolts which was a total waste of time as a hacksaw would have been a more effective tool.

Anyway, next came the handbrake cable, a bit awkward as the clevis pin has to be removed from the handbrake linkage. We were on a four-post ramp so at least had

some room to move. The brake flexible pipe (off-side) was also fiddly but yielded to persistent application. As our car is fitted with ABS, the sensors had to be removed as well. A 10mm screw bolds the sensor to the hub and is easily eased out.

All that was left was the four axle mounts and the radius arms. There was the usual fight in getting the radius arm from the floorpan. One side gave immediately, the other fought and scratched. Eventually, our leverage pulled the rubber away from the centre and, although the arm was free, the steel mount insert was still gripping for all its life. That was despatched with several blows and a cold chisel. And so the axle was out. I left poor Derek to deal with pulling it out and loading it on Alan's van, something Derek was to regret. Although we had removed the axle, it was still on the four-post ramp and it is a hefty, awkward lump.

Strip down

I was astonished to have a call from Alan within a week to say that the axle was ready and where did we want it. The joy about working with Alan is that not only is he extremely competent, he takes his own photographs as well and these, along with his notes saved me a lot of time. Cheers mate.

We had decided not to trust the radius arms, especially as we could obtain complete ready-bushed units from David Manners. This really is a bonus for owners of IRS cars. To have the complete unit available over the counter not only solves the problem of fitting new bushes at home, but means the arm itself, which can be prone to rust, is new as well. All bushes on our car would have had to be replaced anyway as the rubber on one had parted from its steel sleeve.

Alan systematically dismantled the assembly and then started to find more damage. Astonishingly, the near-side lower wishbone had bent at the yolk but we had taken the precaution of getting in a replacement. One universal joint cover had also suffered but this could be beaten back to shape. Both brake discs were due for replacement and the calipers would be rebuilt as a matter of course, as would replacing the shock absorbers.

First off is the shock absorbers/coil springs and those radius arms. Shock absorbers are held with bolts top and bottom but a sleeve is fitted to the top eye and a spacer washer between the shock absorber and wishbone at the bottom. A special half cut (wish I was!) bolt head is used to secure the radius arm. It is made this way to clear the shock absorber tube in the lower wishbone.

When removing the hub carrier, a dummy shaft is inserted in place of the bottom fulcrum shaft. The measurement is exactly that of the distance between the lower wishbone yolk. The idea is that the dummy is tapped through so that when the bottom shaft is pushed out, the dummy retains the bearings, spacers and shims intact. A large nut is removed from the end of the drive shaft (after removing the split-pin). The tightness of this nut does not determine the correct end-float, this is done by shims behind the hub bearing. The drive-shaft itself is held to the output shaft by four nuts (also securing the disc and is spaced with shims for rear camber) while the caliper is wire-bolted to a carrier that itself is bolted to the diff. Across the bottom of the cage is a bottom plate and with this removed, better access is gained. The lower wishbone pivots on an inner shaft and with this pushed through, the wishbone is free.

That just leaves the diff. Bolts pass through the top of the cage to hold the unit in place. These are wired together as it is known for them to shake loose. Another common problem is fatigue across the top of the cage where large

Although showing some slight wear, the inner fulcrum bearing tubes were still in good condition. They were replaced as a precaution, however.

The universal joint cover received some damage but was repairable and would be used again.

A definite candidate for replacement whether the axle had been stripped or not, these discs are in pretty poor condition.

Here's a fault that was unlikely to have been caused by the collision. This outer fulcrum bearing track has cracked. Our work in this area was well timed.

Every item has now been stripped from the cage. The differential unit was the last to be removed seen here with the vacant hole for the electronic speedometer pick up.

The replacement frame was meanwhile being shot-blasted to remove surface rust and grime. It was immediately coated in protective primer.

Removing the caliper mounting bolts was an extremely tricky affair due to the close proximity of the diff. Casing. All are lock-wired.

These are the shims used between the output shaft and drive shaft to determine rear camber.

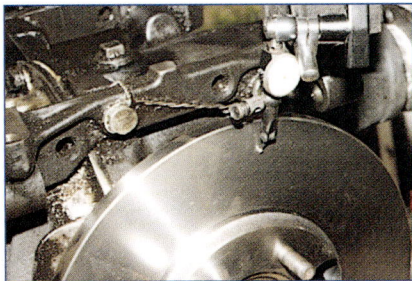

18

A check was made using a dial gauge on the disc to determine if there is any 'run out'.

19

Shims are fitted between the caliper and carrier to ensure that the caliper sits equidistant over the disc. All bolts are then secured with lock wire.

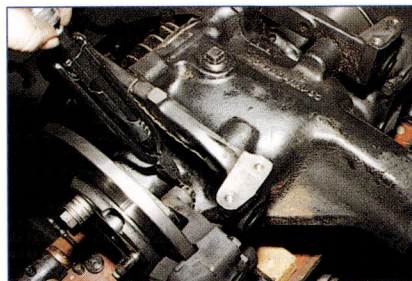

20

Differential, discs and calipers are mounted in the frame.

21

New needle bearings are pressed into the inner fulcrums on the lower wishbone.

22

With the bearing tube installed, thrust washer, seal retaining ring, seal and seal seat are ready for fitting.

23

Lower wishbone has been re-fitted and the drive shaft tightened. Here, the new universal joints are being greased

24

Two halves of the universal joint covers are pop-riveted together.

25

A Jubilee clip holds the end of the cover to the shaft and tightened when the grease nipple is in line with the grease gun hole. A cover is fitted over the hole.

XJS PROJECT

splits can occur.

Assembly as they say, is a reversal of the removal procedure except that we were using new parts throughout. We obtained new shock absorbers from David

Manners and fitting them involved using a spring clamp to compress the coils. The shock absorber is held in place by a couple of collets. In a kind world these are flipped out with a screwdriver but in the real world, they jam and stick but do eventually. Once out, the old damper is slipped out and the new put in its place. With the collets fitted, the compressor can be released. If you do this at home, make sure that you have the right equipment or if you are unsure, have a workshop do it for you - springs hold a lot of energy and are dangerous.

The picture gallery shows the sequence of events on our car.

For a copy of the Jaguar World XK Engine book containing the IRS section, contact the editorial office on 01708 475993.

Acknowledgements:
Bodywork by:
The Romford Bodyshop,
11 Maldon Road, Crow Lane,
Romford, Essex RM7 0JB.
Tel: 01708 723745.
Parts from:
David Manners,
991 Wolverhampton Road,
Oldbury, West Midlands B69 4RJ,
tel: 0121 544 4040, fax: 544.
IRS rebuilds by Alan Slawson on
01277 624295.

Back on the car and the re-manufactured radius arm from Davis Manners is a perfect fit

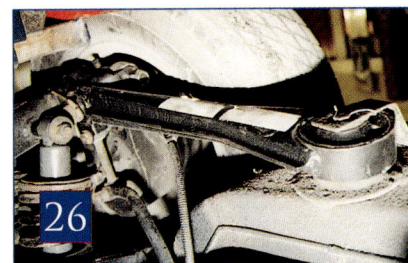

26

XJ-S

In association with
DAVID MANNERS LTD
THE CLASSIC SPECIALIST

PROJECT CAR

Part 5: A Twist in the Tail. Jim Patten tries to find a replacement front axle - and struggles

THE STORY SO FAR:
Part 1 (Vol 10 no 3) - assessment, and removing bumpers, front wings, radiators etc.
Part 2 (Vol 10 no 4) - engine removal, body jigging, body repairs including inner and outer front wings and front panel.
Part 3 (Vol 10 no 5) - body repairs including fitting wings and rear quarter panel, inner wing repairs etc.
Part 4: (Vol 10 no 6) rear axle rebuild.
Part 5: (Vol 10 no 7) rear axle rebuild.

THE CAR:
XJ-S 3.6 coupe manufactured 1988, VIN: SAJJNAEC3CA15441,
purchased as damaged write-off December 1997.
Objective: repair, restore, run and upgrade

Big and beefy does not necessarily mean mighty and strong. Most things have a weakness. Like one of my uncles for instance. High ranking in jujitsu and one of the strongest men I had ever seen (well that's how I remember him from the age of 7). But show him a hypodermic needle and he would collapse a quivering wreck.

The front suspension beam on the XJ-S (and saloon - they're interchangeable) is an enormous girder and is often mistaken for a missing link on the Severn Bridge. Slide into a kerb at an awkward angle, though, and the chances are that the beam will bend. They rust badly too. Predictably, ours had bent so we thought it easier to cast around for a replacement. Alan Duke of XJS Spares (01992 768007) sorted out a seemingly good, straight replacement - or so we both thought. I got stuck in a stripped it down only to find serious rust in the spring turret. It's now resting in peace supporting the concrete base of my motorbike shed. Then Paul Banham came up with a better one,

The upper shock absorber fitting is held by a nut and lock-nut. A wrench on the square end can be used to stop the damper from turning.

A 10mm set-screw holds the **ABS** sensor in place. The sensor can jam so take great care in trying to extract it as damage could occur.

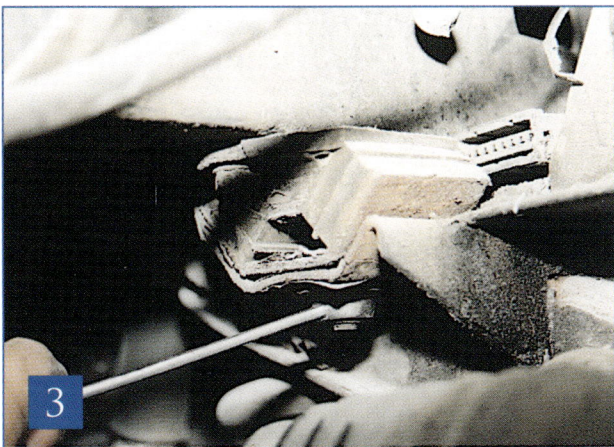

The rear V-mount is undone from inside the engine bay. These can separate without giving a clue as the weight of the car holds everything together. Quite disturbing really! Check by jacking the car and letting the frame hang.

Two brackets hold the anti-roll bar to the car. Undo the bolts and remove. The bushes can be discarded as they will be replaced.

straight, no rust and painted. We were in finally business.

Out with the old

When we started dismantling the car's original beam we couldn't really be sure what components were useable - a pity because everything looked in very good condition. We were safe with the brake calipers, road springs and steering rack. Less certain was the wishbones and hub uprights. At this stage, we didn't realise that the first replacement beam we obtained was rusted and went about stripping that down too. It wasn't a totally wasted effort because we needed its top and bottom wishbones anyway. On our 'replace whatever' list were the shock absorbers, brake discs

and pads as well as all wishbone rubber bushes and ball-joints. These were duly ordered from David Manners and through the mail order service arrived in plenty of time. It pays to order ahead and save the last minute problems.

First job, though, was to extract the damaged beam, easier now that the engine had been removed. We worked from inside the engine bay, first disconnecting the steering column from the rack followed by the hydraulic steering rack pipes. Both shock absorbers were undone at their top mounts and then, moving across to the anti-roll bar mounts, both brackets were released from the body. From inside the engine bay, the rear sub-frame mounts could also be accessed and were soon off. A 10mm bolt held the ABS sensor where it

Beneath the wheel-arch, the brake pipe can be disconnected. A drip tray was placed beneath the pipe to catch the spillage that seemed to go on forever.

First to be removed from the front beam is the anti-roll bar as it was flopping around and just getting in the way.

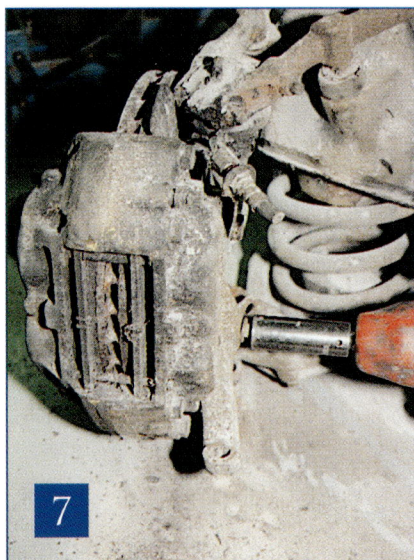

Each caliper is held by two bolts, one of which passes through a steering arm. Disregard the shims that will be fitted between the caliper and upright.

With the rack mount bolts removed, the steering rack can be lifted out. Note that engine mounts vary between models - always check.

A split-pin keeps the hub nut in place. Once undone the hub/disc assembly can be removed as an item.

This is the only safe way to compress the road springs. Jaguar specify a knuckle jointed spring compressor. The Jaguar Enthusiast Club offer them for sale.

The compressor passes through the spring lower seat pan. We had to lightly 'wipe' the hole to get the compressor through.

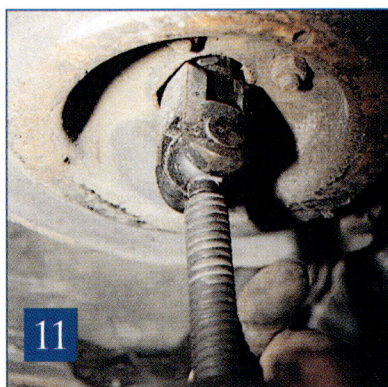

passed through the back of the brake. Sometimes this can be difficult but ours came out quite readily.

Hopping out and moving beneath the wheel-arch, we disconnected the hydraulic brake pipes. Finally, to the front where the sub-frame is held by two doughnut mounts. One of these had already been taken off when the car was straightened. Using jacks and muscle, the beam was eventually pulled out and laid before our feet.

Stripped to the bones

Both beams now had to be stripped bare and re-assembled with straight parts. The peripherals came off easily enough. First came the anti-roll bar as it was flopping around and just got in the way. Next, the shock absorbers were undone by removing the one bolt through the bottom bracket. The brake caliper is held by two bolts with centralising shims. There's absolutely no point in retaining the shims as they will have rusted and disfigured. One of these bolts travels through the steering arm, and by removing the other steering arm bolt, the arm becomes free and saves disturbing the track

rod ends on the steering rack. The disc and hub are held by a large nut with a split pin and once removed, the dust shield is accessible. The small nut holding the shield to the upright is always corroded so it pays to soak it in penetrating oil and then moving the nut back and forth to get it started. Removing the steering rack was achieved by undoing the bolts from the rack mounts and then just lifting away.

Extracting the road springs can be a very hazardous operation as they are held under tremendous tension and we don't advise the amateur to mess around with them unless experienced in this work. Jaguar produced a special tool for the job, a knuckle jointed spring compressor with a positive top location. This is the only tool worth considering if you value your limbs. We borrowed one from E H Autos (01277 631942) but please don't ask, this was a very special favour. Eric does not lend out tools. But the Jaguar Enthusiast Club will sell you one. Try Roger Brotton on 01226 740754.

With the shock absorber removed from the centre of the spring, the tool is offered up through the bottom where a base plate nestles on the lower pan. A spacer fits at the top where two

XJS PROJECT

A couple of prongs on the compressor spacer locate in the front beam turret. This gives a positive location for the compressor.

Once fully wound up, the bolts securing the lower pan can be removed.

Sometimes a bolt might shear. We were able to replace the wishbone but a machine shop should be able to sort the problem out.

prongs locate in recesses in the top of the spring turret. Once positioned and secured, the compressor is gradually wound up until such time as the pressure is taken off the wishbones. The lower plate retaining bolts can then be removed. We had the misfortune of having two shear, leaving the remains stuck in the wishbone. Luckily, we did have a spare wishbone so did not have to start drilling out the remnants. With all bolts removed, the compressor is slackened off allowing the lower pan and thus the spring, to go with it. Note that a nylon spring seat is fitted for the spring to rest on.

Almost home but one last hurdle to cross: removing the wishbones. The tops fought a little due to seized bolts but with plenty of freeing oil, they soon gave. It was curious to see that on one side, a camber shim had not been picked up by its bolt and was simply sitting alongside. That must have made for some interesting suspension angles. The bottoms were a different situation altogether. A fulcrum shaft passes through the beam with castellated nuts (Nyloc on later cars) and split pins at each end. The pins came out okay and the nuts were undone but getting the shaft out was a real nightmare. Water ingress had caused the shaft to bond with the steel inserts of the suspension bushes. We sprayed down the shaft with penetrating oil and then used a soft faced hammer to get things moving. No chance. Eventually one gave but the other had to be sacrificed just to get it out. The luxury of two beams meant we had a replacement as these shafts are not cheap when bought new.

Finally, the wishbones were separated from the upright by releasing the ball-joints. The top first, allowing access to the bottom. As we were replacing the joints, we could take the hooligan route and use a wedge type splitter. It's an incredibly effective tool but destroys everything in its wake. The small edge of the wedge is placed between the joint and then all frustrations can be directed through the hammer as blows are mercilessly delivered. There's little resistance and the joint breaks but part of the joint will have been damaged and the rubber boot torn.

Gosh, is that the time? Must pack up now. All of the parts will be left to soak in degreaser and then it's time for a cup of cocoa and off to bed. Sorry to leave you on the edge of your seat and I realise that the excitement will be almost too much to bear but next month will soon come when we re-assemble the front suspension.

A wedge type ball-joint splitter destroys everything before it but if you are replacing joint and boot, then it really doesn't matter.

When we removed one top wishbone it was noticed that two shims were fitted on the left, just one to the right with its mate floating.

The lower fulcrum shaft was firmly stuck in place. Only one side came out without damage, the other was sacrificed and had to be replaced.

XJ-S PROJECT CAR

In association with

DAVID MANNERS LTD
THE CLASSIC SPECIALIST

Part 6: The twist straightens as Jim Patten puts the front suspension together.

THE STORY SO FAR:
Part 1 (Vol 10 no 3) - assessment, and removing bumpers, front wings, radiators etc.
Part 2 (Vol 10 no 4) - engine removal, body jigging, body repairs including inner and outer front wings and front panel.
Part 3 (Vol 10 no 5) - body repairs including fitting wings and rear quarter panel, inner wing repairs etc.
Part 4: (Vol 10 no 6) rear axle rebuild.
Part 5: (Vol 10 no 7) rear axle rebuild.

THE CAR:
XJ-S 3.6 coupe manufactured 1988, VIN: SAJJ-NAEC3CA15441,
purchased as damaged write-off December 1997.
Objective: repair, restore, run and upgrade

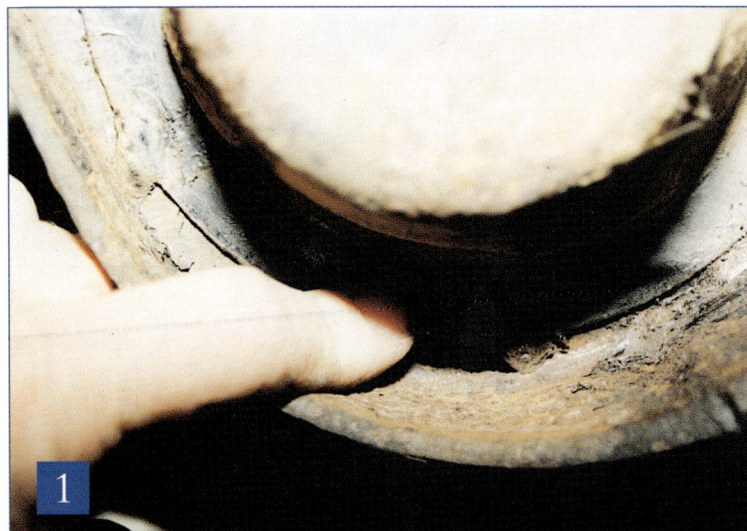

1

Tucked up beneath the front suspension beam turret, the spring seat on our first replacement beam had rusted through.

Time is no respecter of events and as I write this feature I am actually now using our Project XJ-S. It drives arrow straight too, which must be a credit to Derek Swinger's work. If nothing else, it shows that there is a happy ending to this tale. But for now, we're back wielding spanners trying to get the front beam with all its suspension and steering parts rebuilt and back in the car. Essentially, it's a straightforward reversal of the removal procedure with the following additions.

On the bench

Back home on the bench, each wishbone was given a good clean up and then the bushes were removed. I have no fancy kit so used the vice and a couple of old sockets for the bottom bush. One was placed behind the bush, large enough for the old bush to push through. The other was slightly smaller than the bush diameter so that it could push the bush through. Using more penetrating oil

28

2

A couple of old sockets were used to press out the lower wishbone bush. The larger one acted to receive the bush while the smaller one did the pushing.

3

See the difference in the original bush compared to the replacement. Worn bushes not only give a soggy feel to the car's handling, but the suspension geometry can be effected too.

4

Top wishbone bushes are simply levered out of the arm after the arm has been pulled from the wishbone shaft.

on the rubber, the vice was wound up until the bushes popped out.

The inside of the wishbone was thoroughly cleaned before fitting the new bushes. This was done by reversing the removing process. It's important that the bush is fitted exactly central in the wishbone with the same amount of rubber showing at each end. The top is slightly different in that the rubber bush is replaced by a sleeve and collar arrangement. The old ones are levered out and the new pushed in. Quite easy really.

Now it was time to clean up the stub-axle carrier and have a good look at the stub axle. Few people bother to check this out but the stub axle can acquire considerable wear in the region where the inner bearing sits. One of ours was deemed to be too badly worn so we used a better second-hand one that we just happened to have in our now-vast stock. David Manners does supply new ones however. Next, the bottom ball-joints were removed. Ours were the later sealed type and felt good but we replaced them anyway. Four bolts secure it in place and fitting the new joint was routine.

Shims are fitted between the top ball-joint and the wishbone. When the ball-joint was removed, the shims were marked and stored so that they could be re-fitted to the appropriate area. There is no chance that they will give the correct

suspension reading but it does provide a datum point. Again, a new top ball-joint was used. The roll-bar was undamaged and it too had new rubber mounts fitted. We did consider fitting polyurethane bushes but decided to stick with the original type. The whole thing was assembled using a splash of black paint to brighten things up a bit.

On the braking front, the calipers were sent off to be reconditioned while I rebuilt the hubs. The five bolts securing the disc to the hub were removed first and the disc removed. All traces of grease was removed from the hub (mucky!) and the bearing tracks tapped out with a long drift. Any rough burrs were filed off using a fine file. Diving into the old socket box, I found a couple of sockets the same diameter as the two bearing tracks. Laying the tracks in position, the socket was used to tap the tracks home. Ideally a press should be used as they do need considerable force to get them pushed all the way.

The new discs come with a protective layer of grease which should be cleaned off with thinners. With the face of the hub thoroughly cleaned too (any high spots will effect braking), the new disc was offered up and the bolts fully tightened to a torque of 41-54 Nm.

Back to the stub axle carrier and the new lower ball-joint: if you are converting from the old

5

Thrust washers and bush are removed from the top wishbone shaft. The bush had worn and would have been noticeable by a clonk from the front or vague steering.

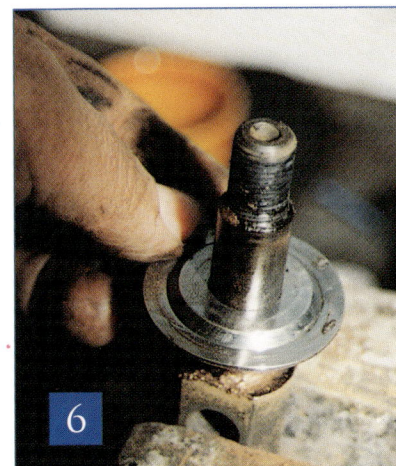

6

Building up the top wishbone by first fitting the outer thrust washer using Copper Ease on the outside.

7

Top wishbone bushes follow. Note that the inner bush is already lubricated. The arm is placed over the inner bush, followed by the outer bush and washers. The nut is not fully tightened until the suspension is back on the car and the full weight applied.

8

Always check the stub axle for wear around the bearing track area. This one was judged to be too worn and was replaced. David Manners keep new stub axles in stock.

New sealed for life bottom ball-joints were used. If these are replacements for the earlier type, four shorter securing bolts will be needed.

9

When fitting the top ball-joint, the shims were replaced as they came out. A proper geometry check and adjust will be made later.

10

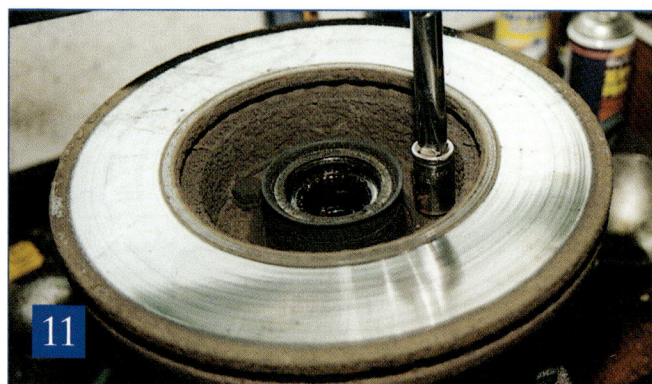

11

Five bolts hold the brake disc to the hub. Dirt builds up around the bolts making it difficult to locate the socket. Always clean the area - burr these bolts at your peril.

type ball-joint with shims, then remember that new shorter bolts will be needed. Ours was a straightforward replacement.

Nothing was wrong with the rack and pinion steering so it was just cleaned up and fitted with new bushes. I used the tool obtained from Classic Spares (01992 716236) for our Series 3 XJ6. It's so easy to use, enabling the bushes to be changed with the rack still on the car if needed. Basically, a cylindrical section is positioned over the bush and a threaded rod passed though into a receiving washer the other side. As the thread is tightened, so the bush is pulled out. To replace, the system is reversed and the new bush pulled into the rack.

Back together again

Having rejected the first replacement front axle beam on the grounds of rust in the turret, we turned to the newly painted one supplied by Paul Banham. The newly bushed lower wishbone was fitted with (remembering the removal problems) the cross-shaft covered in Comma CopperEase. The nuts we used were the later Nyloc type, avoiding the split pins. Up at the top, the wishbone was connected to the top turret using the shims that we took out. The top-ball joint was assembled to the wishbone arm using the shims we removed, steering alignment would be done later.

'Our' spring compressor came into play again, this time to load up the lower pan and get the spring compressed so that the bolts would re-unite it to the lower wishbone arms. Once all bolts were fitted and tightened, the compressor was removed.

Always use the right equipment and take great care with road springs - if in doubt leave this job to an expert. The disc back plate followed and then the disc/hub assembly with the relevant seals and bearings. All bearings were fully greased with LM grease, placed on their tracks and then the grease seal was fitted. This is offered up to the stub axle and secured with the nut. An end float of 0.03-0.08mm is ideal but most people just tighten the nut up and back off by one flat of the bolt. The bolt cover and split pin is then fitted. The bearing end-float must be re-checked once the car has done 50 miles or so.

Refitting the calipers is a delicate affair. Shims are provided to get the caliper body central over the disc. It's fiddly and irritating. Sometimes it's done first time, at others it take forever. Finally tighten to 68-91Nm. When fitting the steering rack,

A slot is located beneath the bearing track. Working from the other side, a long drift is used to tap the bearing track out.

In the absence of press facilities, a socket the identical size of the bearing track is used to tap the bearing track into the hub.

New brake discs are coated with a film of light grease. Clean it off using a degreaser or thinners.

shims are provided to take up any free play between the mounts and the bracket on the sub-frame. There is a whole paragraph on setting the rack on the sub frame but it can be short circuited by aligning the rack in parallel to the sub-frame (IE, visually look at the gap between the rack and the edge of the frame). Note that by the time our XJ-S was built, stiffer rack mountings were standard so make sure that if you replace them, you get the correct type - they make a difference.

Getting the assembly back on the car is very much a reversal of the removal procedure. The dampers will be left until the under bonnet is painted (less to mask up) and the wishbone nuts will not be fully tightened until the car is on the floor under its full weight when a torque of 43-68Nm lower and 61-75Nm upper will be used.

One final point to remember. If you do use a different front beam, always use the engine mount brackets to suit the engine - they're all different.

Next Month: Putting on the primer

The hub nut is tightened until the bearing is in full contact with the track. It is then backed of a quarter of a turn and the split-pin fitted.

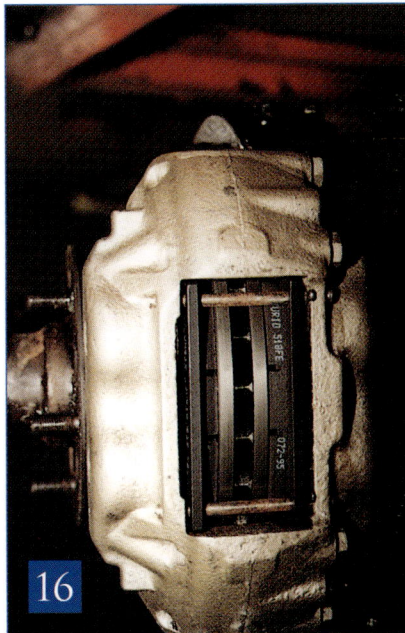

Shims are provided between the caliper and bracket . They are added or subtracted until the caliper sits centrally over the disc.

The steering rack bush removal tool marketed by Classic Spares is used to draw the bushes out without any fuss.

XJ-S
PROJECT CAR

In association with

DAVID MANNERS LTD
THE CLASSIC SPECIALIST

Part 7: Top coat - Jim Patten returns to the Romford Bodyshop

THE CAR:
XJ-S 3.6 coupe manufactured 1988, VIN: SAJJNAEC3CA15441,
purchased as damaged write-off December 1997.
Objective: repair, restore, run and upgrade

THE STORY SO FAR:

Part 1 (Vol 10 no 4) assessment and removing bumpers, front wings, radiator etc.
Part 2: (VOl 10 no 5) engine removal, body jigging, body repairs including inner and outer front wings and front panel.
Part 3: (Vol 10 no 6) - panelling up, fitting front wings, bonnet and rear quarter panel. Part 4: (Vol 10 no 7) rear axle rebuild.
Part 5: (Vol 10 no 8) front suspension strip
Part 6: (Vol 10 no 9) front suspension rebuild

Derek Swinger at the Romford Bodyshop is now shot of Jaguar World personnel as the XJ-S is now painted. Up until then, the only chance he's had to be alone is in the spray booth and even then, I dived in, breath held, to freeze the moment on film. But take care - the modern two-pack paint mix is pretty obnoxious and you should never be anywhere near the spray fall-out minus proper breathing apparatus.

The primer is on and now the guide coat is being applied. Any different colour can be used. Derek always has a quantity of dregs laying around in the bottom of cans, perfect for this task.

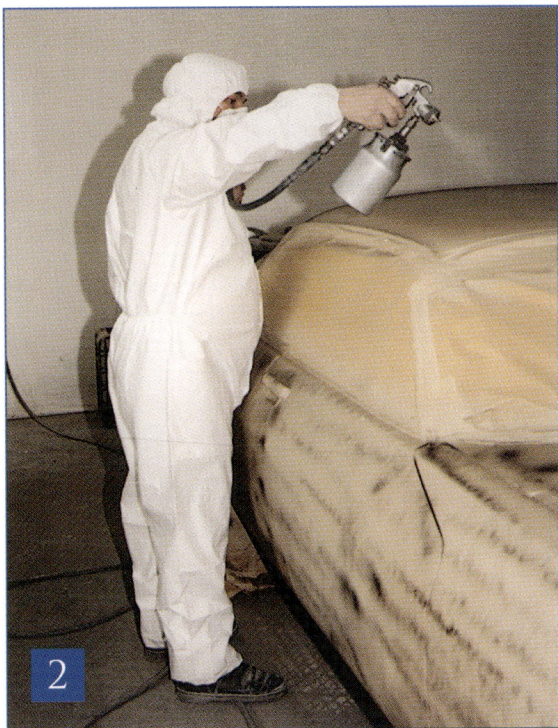

2

The slog continues as the guide coat is taken back. The idea is to remove every trace of paint and get back to the primer. In theory, there should be no imperfections.

3

Despite all of Derek's efforts to eradicate the dust, these marks shown up by the guide coat were probably caused by the traitorous specks.

4

Finally, the two-pack top coat is applied. The breathing apparatus Derek is wearing is fed by a separate air source, taken from outside the oven, as indeed is the air for spraying.

Preparation

Derek put both axles back in the car to get it mobile again. It is possible to manoeuvre the shell around on a wheeled jig but it can still be cumbersome. Re-fitting is a reversal of the removal process, only much easier as there are no nasty seized nuts and bolts to remove. Liberal applications of CopperEase were applied to all fixing bolts and especially to the radius arm dome mount on the rear floor-pan. Such consideration for the next generation who may restore this car again; just shows how we think at JW.

Right, on to the cosmetics. Derek had achieved the flattest possible surface he possibly could with a lengthy application of body filler and then, in the universal fashion, flattened the whole lot back until the body appeared dead straight. Various grades of 3M wet & dry production paper were used, the later ones taking out the scratch lines left by earlier, coarse papers. Most of the filler ended up on the shop floor but what did remain was critical in eradicating minor flaws and low points (not rust, of course - all that had been dealt with as we have explained) to achieve those perfectly straight flanks.

The clean up job has to be thorough beyond reckoning. First, all of the fallen dust is vacuumed before the body is tackled with clinical efficiency. Dust will find a hiding place in every little crevice so a blow jet on the air-line chases it out of each hiding place, an exercise repeated time and time again as Murphy's Law dictates that dust from one crack will find a home in another.

On with the paint

Satisfied that the car is dust-free, every part not to be painted has to be masked up. Derek uses 3M masking tape and paper for this as some cheaper tapes can lift and therefore becomes self-defeating. This applies to some under-bonnet areas too as spray 'dust' can get in through the grille opening. Masking up takes place in the low-bake oven and while the shell is subjected to a slow heat to take the chill off it, Derek mixed his two-pack primer. Whatever paint you chose, always follow the manufacturer's instructions to the letter. Derek applied the primer to fully cover the car with sufficient depth to allow for flattening but not too much to give the opportunity of cracking. Using 1000 grade 3M wet and dry paper, wet, the entire car was flattened to take off the as-sprayed finish. It was now ready for a guide coat. This is a coat of any contrasting colour lying around. The idea is to afterwards flatten again which will reveal any imperfections, as the 'guide' paint will lie in shallows. These can then be filled with body stopper. Any imperfections will be of tiny pro-

5

Will it ever end? Derek is back with his bucket and wet 3M paper as he hand flats every square inch of the XJ-S.

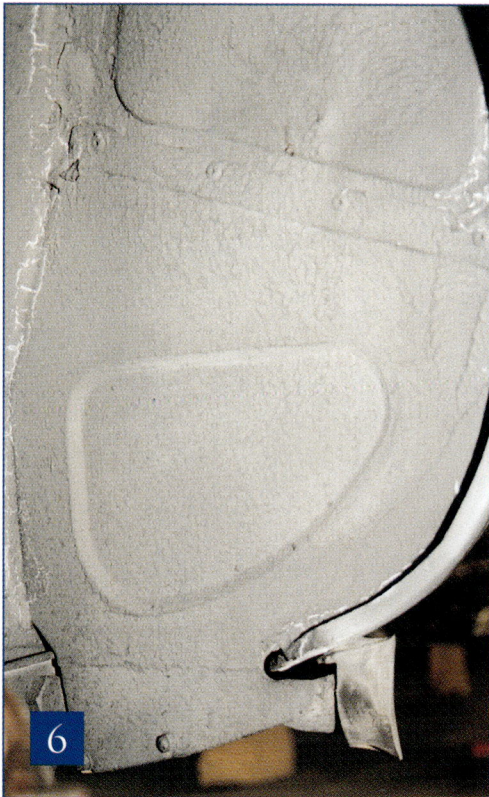

6

7

(6) The inside of the wheel-arch has been re-sealed around the wing edge using 3M sealer and then sprayed over with under-body compound. A full rust proofing will follow, a procedure we will show in detail.

(7) Back with the bumpers. David Manners supplied a new inner bumper support member as the old one had fallen victim to the accident. Brackets were straightened out though.

portions but make the difference between an okay job and a super job.

So, more flattening with wet 1,000 grade paper until all of the guide coat was removed. A couple of small rectifications were needed and then our XJ-S was ready for colour.

Most finishes these days are a clear lacquer over a colour base. That means a quite coarse coat of paint is applied first and left. It needs to be coarse to act as a key for the lacquer top coat which is applied next. Both are obnoxious two-pack mixes and incredibly dangerous to breath in. Care must be taken not to get any runs in the paint as two-pack is not forgiving - once it goes off, it becomes rock hard and very difficult to cut back. The car was left overnight on a low heat to cure the paint.

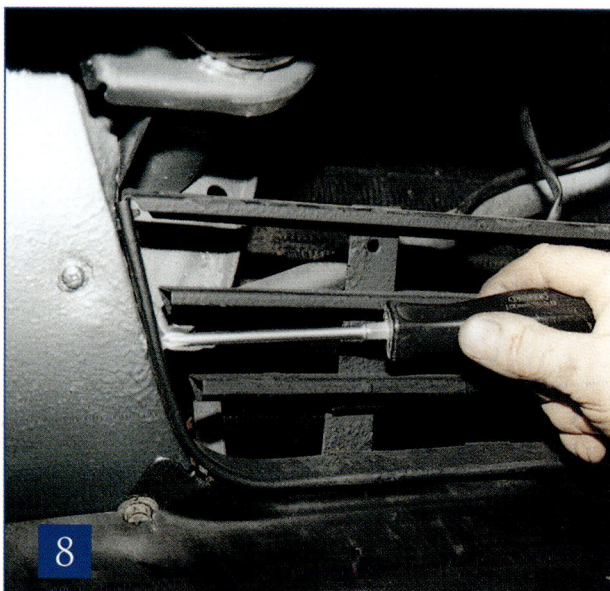

8

Miraculously, this lower grille came through unscathed. New screws and clips were used however.

Now if you think the foregoing was hard, you ain't seen nuffin' yet! As hinted, this paint sets hard by chemical reaction rather than by the evaporating of solvents. If applied by an expert the finish 'from the gun' is adequate and many modern cars leave the factory sprayed to this standard. Not Jaguar though. Derek got stuck in with 1200 grade 3M paper, wet, and flattened the whole car. Then he attacked it with the mop and compound. This is a fine abrasive which follows on from the paper. Once that had been done, a hand glaze is applied to put the shine into the car.

There you are, it's a simple as that. Now toddle off and do your own. All you need is thousands of pounds worth of equipment, an oven, breathing apparatus, a bucket full of skill and years of experience. Good luck!

It's a fit-up, guv!

Engine back first or shall we do the tinsel? We wanted to see our newly painted car with chrome so we decided tinsel. We had a great big box with David Manners stickers all over it and we were like children opening up our presents. New headlights - wow! New front bumper corner - oh, boy! The grille was re-usable and was simply screwed in place. One precaution we'd taken was to order up all new screws, clips and fasteners. So many break during removal, or are unsightly. The lot came to no more than around £10, an insignificant sum for the convenience.

It is now that the value of trial-fitting pays off. Whenever Derek undertakes any restoration or accident damage work, he always asks for the lights, bumpers and any other relevant fittings up front. If, say, a headlight or bumper does not fit correctly before primer stage, Derek can make the necessary adjustments without prejudicing a shiny top-coat. As it was, everything was easy. New side-repeater lights were supplied through David Manners. These never come out intact so, being our ever considerate selves, CopperEase was applied during fit up.

At the front, the centre bumper and near-side bumper blades

XJS PROJECT

The lights and surrounds fitted perfectly but then, Derek had taken great pains in trial fitting them earlier in the repair operations.

Quite how the grille escaped is one of those unanswerable questions but it is being re-fitted here. New number plates were needed.

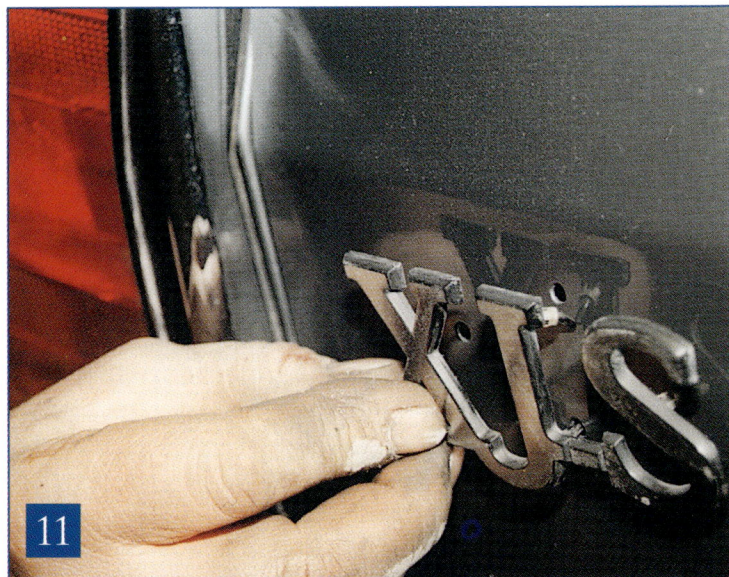

Nothing wrong with the badges as they were all in quite good condition and eminently re-usable. Even the clips were intact.

were okay. But we did need a replacement off-side blade and better rubber. We obtained a good second-hand rubber from Paul Banham and were impressed by the chrome match of the new bumper to the existing. Obviously, our XJ-S has been cared for. At the back, a replacement off-side bumper blade and lower rubber were needed. I actually had a spare. It came with the spares cache when I bought the silver Series 2 XJ6.

It was all coming together. Rear lights were re-used and the electric aerial re-fitted. Number plates were made up for us by our friend John Lane at Motorways Auto Stores (0181 592 0294). Door handles were re-fitted (if you do this, take great care as over-tightening can cause a couple of dimples on the door skin as the securing bridge forces its way into the metal).

All was looking good and showed the value of replacing any second-rate 'jewellery' - new paint will tend to make items which previously were quite passable look decidedly second-hand.

Well, next month we'll pop the engine and transmission back in (by we I mean Derek, of course). Then we should be running.

Electric aerial and rear lights were simply put back. At this stage we did not know if the aerial would work. We later discovered it to be perfectly good.

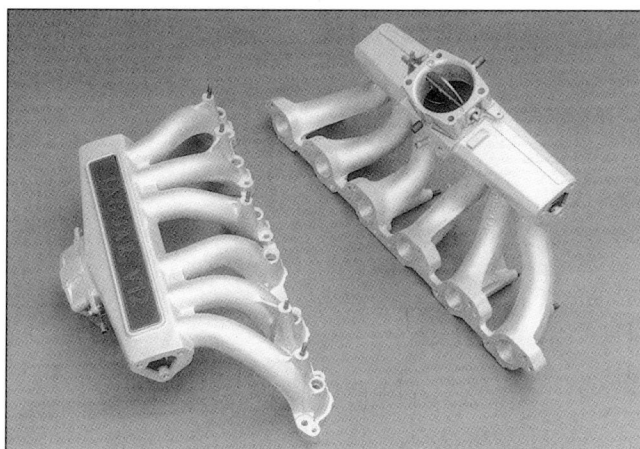

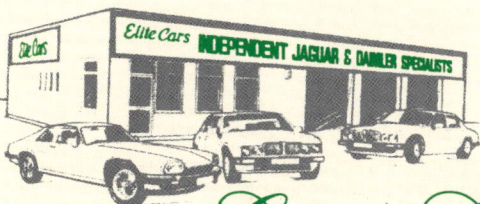

XJ-S

In association with

DAVID MANNERS LTD
THE CLASSIC SPECIALIST

PROJECT CAR

Part 8: Putting the engine back. Jim Patten watches the return of the power plant.

THE CAR:
XJ-S 3.6 coupe manufactured 1988, VIN: SAJJNAEC3CA15441, purchased as damaged write-off December 1997.
Objective: repair, restore, run and upgrade

THE STORY SO FAR:
Part 1 (Vol 10 no 4) - assessment and removing bumpers, front wings. Radiator etc.
Part 2 (Vol 10 no 5) - engine removal, body jigging, body repairs including inner and outer front wings and front panel.
Part 3 (Vol 10 no 6) - panelling up, fitting front wings, bonnet and rear quarter panel.
Part 4 (Vol 10 no 7) - rear axle rebuild.
Part 5 (Vol 10 no 8) - rear axle rebuild continued.
Part 6 (Vol 10 no 9) - front suspension removal and strip.
Part 7 (Vol 10 no 10) - painting the body

1

Easy does it. Will full control at a touch of a button, Derek Swinger eased our 3.6 AJ6 engine back into the XJ-S.

Our XJ-S is looking like a car again. Our next step is to make it go like one. Nothing had been done to the engine or transmission so we really only intended to clean it up and put it back with new perishables. We will be making one or two upgrades in the future but until then, the car will be left standard. After all, we need to know what the car was like before, so that we can assess the after.

The general condition appeared to be very good and a bit of work with some degreaser and a high pressure hose soon had the engine sparkling. What we originally took to be a crack in

As the engine starts its journey back into the bay, a constant eye must be kept on each side to check that it is running true. One slight slip would result in damage top our fresh paint.

The engine mounts are easily accessed and once they have been located in the engine bracket slots, the weight of the engine can be transferred over to the car.

Everything fails naturally to hand. Here, the harness is being connected along the fuel injection rail.

Throttle cable and return spring find their location. Any adjustments will be done once the car has been brought up to temperature.

an exhaust manifold turned out to be a casting line so we were saved the bother of finding a replacement. While we drained the oils from the engine and transmission, a list was made to be faxed over to David Manners. As well as plugs and filters, we also needed a radiator, air-conditioning condenser, oil cooler and exhaust system. Tragically, the oil cooler was undamaged but as in virtually every case, when the union is undone, the fragile aluminium threads strip, rendering the cooler useless.

I took the cooling fan home as the motor seemed to have seized and thought that a bit of a clean up would do the trick. Was I wrong! Three screws held the end cover of the motor in place and once off, the entire contents fell out in a rusted mass. Apparently, this is quite common as the motor sticks out in the breeze and is open to the elements. With only the genuine (and expensive) original available as an alternative, Derek Swinger came to the rescue just before I went in search of second-hand. He had a new motor on the shelf that was identical. He couldn't recall where it came from but a motor is a motor and as this one was true right down the correct rpm, so that's good enough for us.

Our parcel turned up from David Manners, efficient as ever, loaded with the rest of the goodies. The radiator and condenser would follow as our original items were being reconditioned. They are available exchange but we figured that our original items would be just fine. The damage had not inflected too much harm and the simple twist was easily rectified. And sure enough, when the units did arrive, they were as good as new. The exhaust system also arrived that week. David Manners recommended a Falcon stainless steel system and who are we to argue.

One further complication was the rather bent gearbox mount. We tried in vain to replace the part but got bogged down. Derek just picked up the twisted metal and wandered off in the direction of a friend who had a power press. He sauntered back a little later with a perfectly straight

gearbox mount. How is it that he is able to make everything look so easy? Before installing the engine, Derek removed the bonnet once more to get the access needed to lower the engine in place.

Using the overhead electric winch eased the job of getting the engine/transmission unit back. It has to go in at a bit of angle first and then gradually tilted to raise the tail of the transmission and guide it home. It's best to have a few pairs of eyes available to make sure that the great heavy lump doesn't start crashing into the newly finished paintwork.

As soon as the unit got so far, a trolley jack was positioned on the transmission tailshaft. This was lifted slightly and the engine lowered. Turn after turn the process continued and soon the engine began to find its own way in. There were times when it looked as though it would never go back despite the fact that it came out. Then all of a sudden, the engine was sitting right over the engine mounts. A screwdriver and lever helped get the threaded part of the mount into the engine bracket and once both had penetrated the engine bracket, the engine was lowered down and the weight taken by the car. The trolley jack remained in place for the time being.

Putting all of the wires and fittings back in place easy enough. It was just routine and not difficult at all. Most parts are obvious due to the way the bits and pieces are bent or positioned. Look at any part of the wiring loom and it sort of just falls were it should go. At the end of each section, a multi-plug fits with its mate and is unique. If you find that a section of wire lines up with a part that will not fit, something with the routing is wrong, so check again. For instance, the section of harness that fits along the fuel injection rail simply laid down ready to surrender. The same went for the power steering and air-conditioning pipes. They are all bent in a manner ready to connect to the next section. New cotton real mounts were needed to install the air filter box otherwise the operation went like clockwork.

The radiator and air-conditioning condenser are installed back

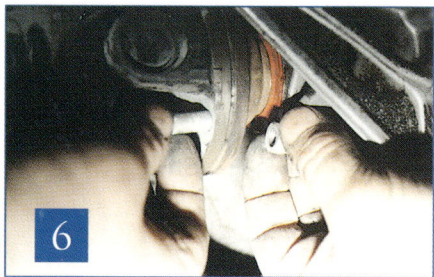

6

The prop-shaft is coupled paying due attention to the marks made to re-align the flanges. Always use new Nyloc nuts.

7

Derek Swinger was able to straighten the rear gearbox mount and found that it fitted back perfectly.

8

Working around the engine bay, the coolant expansion tank is bolted back on to the inner wing.

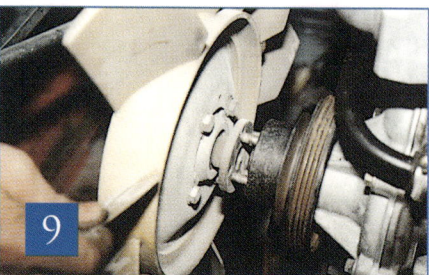

9

The viscous coupling on the fan is thoroughly checked before replacing the unit. Ours was okay.

10

In goes the radiator to be followed by the air conditioning condenser. Everything lined up perfectly. Sighs of relief as it did have a bit of a twist.

11

Like the wiring, all coolant, air conditioning and power steering pipes just fall into place naturally.

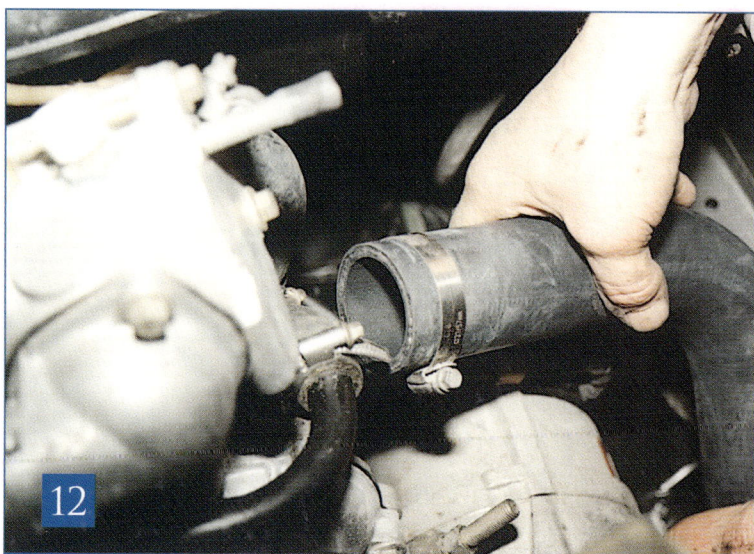

12

New clips were used on hoses that looked almost new. Some money had been spent on this car before we got it.

XJS PROJECT

Continuing around the inner wing, more of the electronics are re-fitted. Luckily, all of these units seem to have escaped damage.

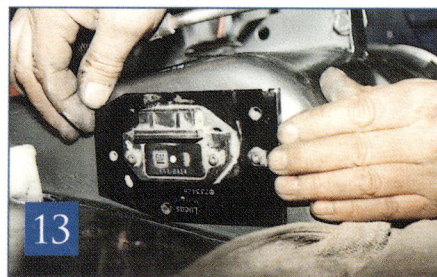

13

to back. That's been a bit of a problem with these and XJ40s as debris falls between the two and causes an air flow problem, effectively strangling the cooling fins. At least ours would be completely clear for a few years. Hoses were coupled and clips fitted and when every multi-plug was plugged and all pipes fitted, Derek went underground.

Having a ramp has so many advantages. Derek just positioned a sturdy piece of timber and blocks below the gearbox and let the jack go. The car was then lifted up on the ramp. We checked the universal joints on the prop-shaft and could find no detectable wear. The shaft went back acknowledging the marks made with office Tippex on the shaft flanges to maintain alignment. New Nyloc nuts and bolts were used for this job. Speedometer wiring and selectors were connected before the transmission mount went on. Our repaired original fitted perfectly.

At last the new exhaust system could go on. Derek had a bit of a fight getting one of the pipes right but a little bit of heat soon had it in place. Each joint was treated to a bit of assembly paste and new clamps. The newly fitted and polished pipes existing the back of the car looked tremendous against the new paint. It's almost a shame to take the car out and get it all weathered.

We chose Comma Coldstream antifreeze. It's a ready mix so you simply tip the contents of the container into the system. It also has the benefit of a higher boiling point than most others. We don't anticipate that sort of need in the XJ-S but most older Jaguars are pretty grateful for those extra couple of degrees.

Engine filled with oil and a measured amount for the gearbox and it was time to fire the XJ-S up. Always a worrying time. Will oil spill out of every crevice? Will water stream issue forth from leaking seams? Only one way to find out. With the battery fully charged, Derek cranked the

A new oil cooler was needed not through damage but because the aluminium threads on the unions had stripped. Only the cotton-real mounts had suffered harm.

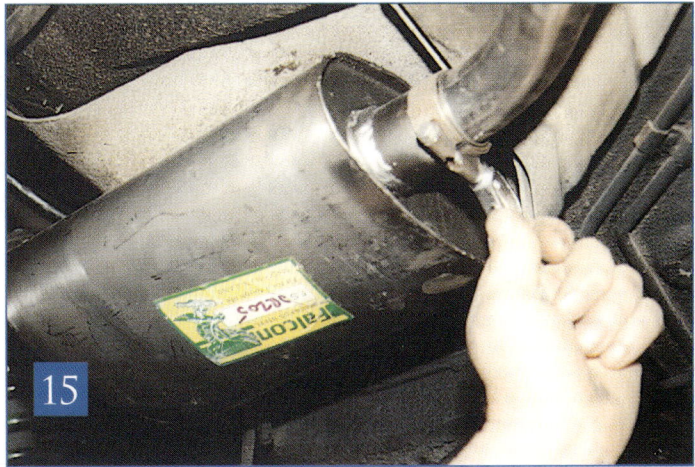

In the main, the Falcon exhaust system was easy to fit and looked terrific against the new paint.

The replacement service items go in at last. Here a new air filter element is fitted into the canister.

The non-turning auxiliary fan that didn't turn. A common problem on the XJ-S.

Look what happened when the fan motor was taken apart. This was beyond any thoughts of saving it and replacement was the only way to go.

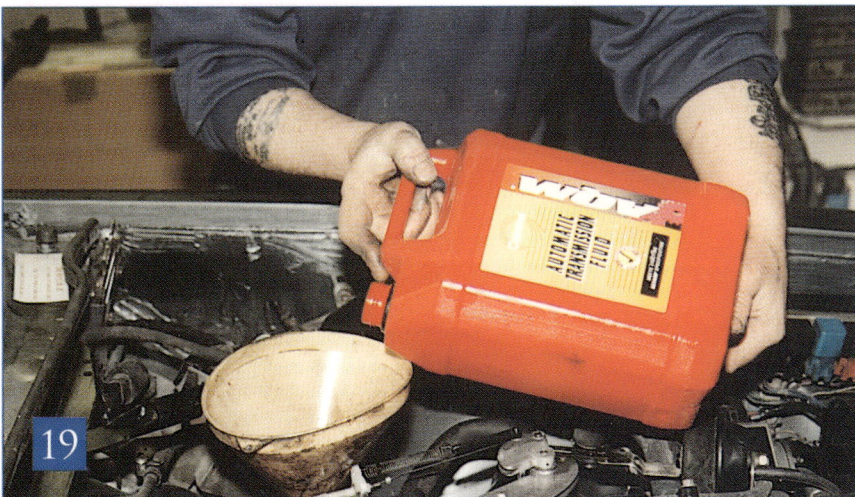

Finally, all oils were poured into the engine, transmission etc. and the engine fired up. We had it running first time.

engine over a few times to get everything primed. The best way to do this on any car is to disconnect an essential wire from a coil or similar vital part. When he tried it for real, the workshop filled with the sounds of an AJ6 engine running on all of its six cylinders. We were nearly there.

Allowing a bit of time for things to cool down (the bonnet went back in that period), Derek filled the fluid reservoir with brake fluid, and using a Sealey bleeding kit that pulled the fluid out of the bleed nipples without need of applying the brake pedal, expelled all air from the system.

Bleeding the later XJ-S is a doddle anyway. It's just a question of running the engine, applying pressure to the brake pedal and cracking each bleed nipple. We had brakes.

The final job was to go around the car to check out for leaks, and fit things like windscreen wipers, check lights, horn and indicators and generally finish off the twiddly bits. Yes, it looks like we are ready for the MoT. But that will have to wait until next month.

XJ-S PROJECT CAR

In association with
DAVID MANNERS LTD
THE CLASSIC SPECIALIST

Part 9: Back on the road again! Jim Patten sorts out the angles

THE STORY SO FAR:

Part 1 (Vol 10 no 4) - assessment and removing bumpers, front wings, radiator etc.
Part 2 (Vol 10 no 5) - engine removal, body jigging, body repairs including inner and outer front wings and front panel.
Part 3 (Vol 10 no 6) - panelling up, fitting front wings, bonnet and rear quarter panel.
Part 4 (Vol 10 no 7) - rear axle rebuild.
Part 5 (Vol 10 no 8) - rear axle rebuild continued.
Part 6 (Vol 10 no 9) - front suspension removal and strip.
Part 7 (Vol 10 no 10) - top coat, resprayed at last.

THE CAR:
XJ-S 3.6 coupe manufactured 1988, VIN: SAJJNAEC3CA15441, purchased as damaged write-off December 1997. Objective: repair, restore, run and upgrade

"You'd better come and pick this car up - don't you think I've had it long enough? Oh yes, it's just passed its MoT too." The dulcet tones of Derek Swinger of the Romford Bodyshop announced that he had finally finished his work. Our XJ-S was a runner again. Somehow, it had lingered longer than we expected but running a magazine mysteriously got in the way. But at last, Derek was free of us. We'll be back though.

Remember, I've a Mk1 saloon that needs sorting.

I must admit to a certain apprehension while on my way to collect the XJ-S - a car that I've never driven and heard running only once. Not only that, it's been repaired after a fairly nasty crash. While I have the greatest confidence in the work that Derek had done, I still had an unreasonable doubt nagging in my mind. And then I saw it. Fully fitted up and polished, it

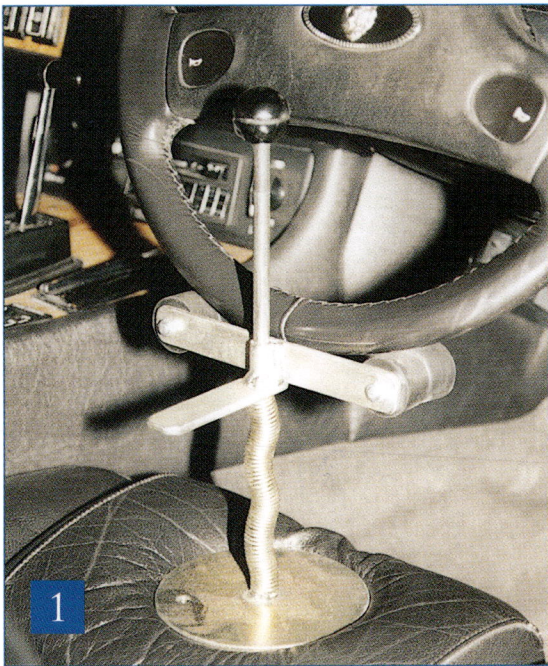

As the steering must be in the straight ahead position at all times, this spring device applies gentle pressure to keep it there.

To keep interaction between all four wheels, a laser is hung on one axle and aimed at the other. This is also a good way to check for true between front and rear.

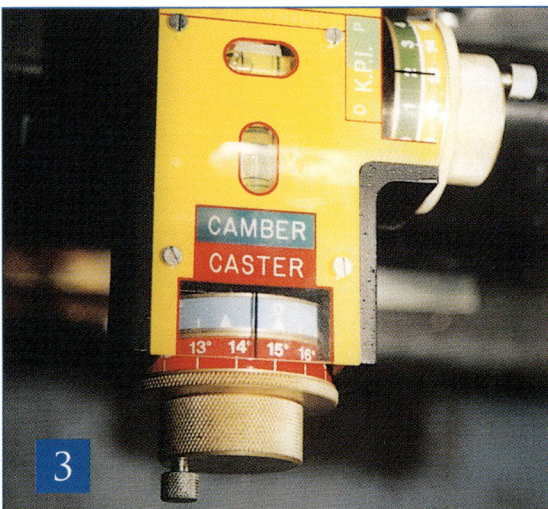

Another device attached to the wheels is this one which checks the camber and castor. Plum line bubbles use gravity to give readings

really did look good on Derek's forecourt.

But of course there was still quite a lot of work to do. Before going anywhere, we had to sort out the steering geometry although Derek had set the tracking so at least we would be able to drive down the road safely. Much more critical, though, the radio wouldn't work because I didn't have the code. I was flattened. I'd brought a couple of tapes along and realised that I would have to drive home without the company of Enigma.

Prioritising the work schedule, I contacted Grange Motors of Brentwood who serviced the car for the previous owner and, after crossing their palm with £10, I had the radio code. Of course, like any dealer, they needed proof of ownership to prevent dirty doings but at last I had music. So I was more relaxed as I drove to Colchester and Smiley's Auto Engineers. They had the job of checking and adjusting the steering geometry.

A lesson in geometry

It seems that unless you have a laser something or other in your toolkit, then you're out of date these days. Smiley's have a four-wheel laser measuring device that not only checks across the car, it does fore and aft as well. Now the great thing with a Jaguar is the ample opportunity for wheel alignment adjustment. On the front, shims on the top wishbone fulcrum shaft take care of camber. More shims between the top ball joint and the wishbone arms sort out the castor while tracking is done in the normal way by adjusting the track rods. At the rear, only camber is adjustable. Shims are fitted between the drive shaft and inboard disc. Further shims are located behind the lower fulcrum shaft inner mounting bracket. So, with all of these variables to play with, it was over to Steve to sort something out for us.

First job was to fix the steering wheel in the straight ahead position. The correct way to make sure that everything is facing front is to insert special tool number 18G 1466 into the steering rack. The suspension should also be locked in mid-laden position but with a three-quarter full fuel tank, the car's own weight should be sufficient. We set the correct tyre pressures (32psi front, 36 rear) and then rolled the car back and forth to let it 'settle'. Once that position was established, a spring device was put between the steering wheel and the seat to hold the wheel firm.

Outside, a laser light was hung on the rear wheel and, in line with it, a scale on the front wheel. Both were adjusted to the upright position and then it was time to switch on the lights. The laser projected forward onto the scale where we found that we were not too far out. Front camber showed 0.25 degree nearside and 0.5 degree negative offside. Castor was 2.5 degrees n/s and 2.5 degree o/s. Tracking has to be checked after these adjustments had been done.

Castor should be 3.5 degrees ± 0.25 degrees positive. We had a full degree on one side and 0.75 on the other to make up. This meant shuffling the shims around, moving from the rear of the ball-joint to the front. Each 1.6mm shim is worth 0.25 degree. By moving four on one wheel and three on the other, we had our castor sorted although we would obviously need to re-check this later. Camber should be 0.5 degree ± 0.25 degree with both wheels within 0.25 degree of each other. We were actually within the given limits. Had we not been, then the bolts securing the inner wishbone shaft should be slackened. Shims measure 0.8mm, 1.6mm and 3.2mm. An addition of 0.25 degree can be added or subtracted by the value of 1.6mm worth of shimming. Always re-tighten the shaft bolts. Camber would wait until the rear adjustments had been done.

Rear adjustments

We already knew that our ride height was correct but if you are doing this on a car where the information is not clear, then a measurement should be taken beneath the rear cage, directly under the lower wishbone inner fulcrum shaft at the lowest level (ie turned edge) of the bottom cage plate. If this is not 190.6 ± 6.4mm, then you should investigate further as wear is likely.

Our laser lights were now reversed and the upright position re-

The camber needed altering on the rear wheel which involved slackening the universal joint shroud. Make sure that when refitting, the grease nipple hole is correctly sited.

With the shroud clear of the inboard flange, the four nuts can be removed to withdraw the halfshaft from the inner hub.

As the shaft is removed, the shims become visible. Each is 0.5mm thick which is worth 0.25 degree on or off camber.

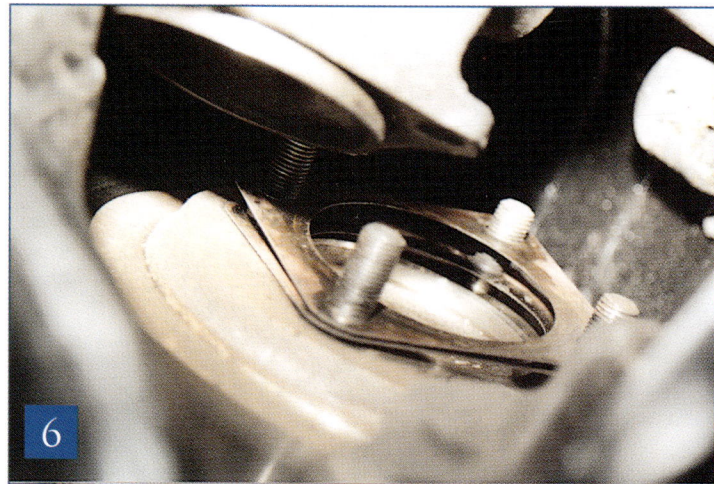

aligned. The correct reading should be 0.75 ± 0.25 degree negative. Miraculously, we were within limits on the near-side but had 1.25 degree on the off-side. Shims are available measuring 0.5mm worth 0.25 degree each. But adjustment now gets messy. These shims are situated between the drive shaft and the inboard disc which involves releasing the four nuts holding the shaft inboard and pulling it away to get shims in or out.

As a precaution, the grease nipple fitted in the aluminium hub carrier is removed. Then, the shroud covering the inboard universal joint is slackened by letting the clips off so that the shroud can be moved back (or completely removed if wished). Now, the four nuts can be seen. They are removed one at a time as the shaft has to be rotated so that they can be accessed. It's actually worth taking all of the shims out

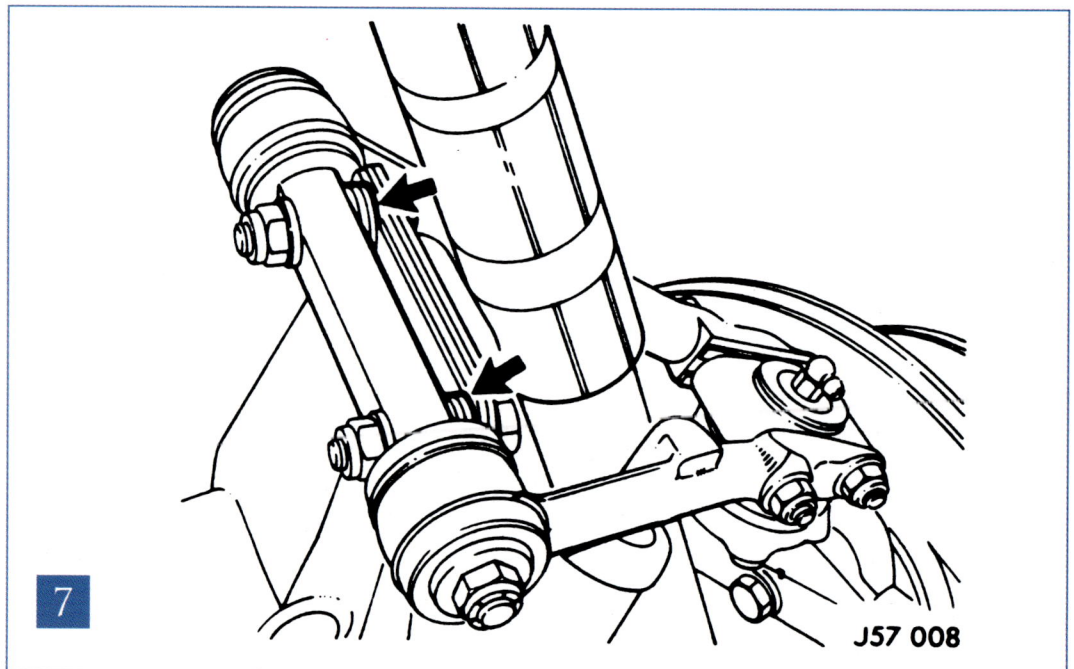

J57 008

Front camber is adjusted by moving shims between the inner top wishbone shaft. Adding increases camber, removing decreases it.

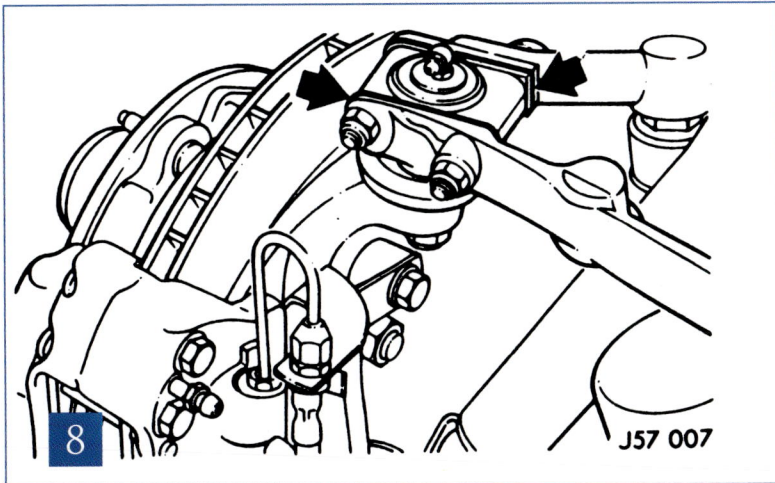

J57 007

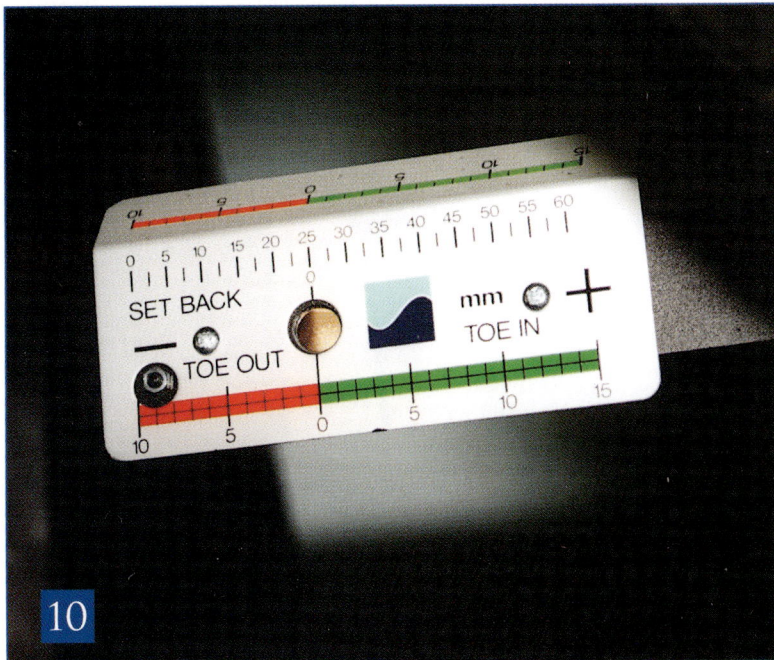

Left: Caster is controlled by use of shims either side of the top ball joint. They can be swopped from front to rear to either increase or decrease caster.

Above: Front wheels are rolled onto a platform that can turn with the wheels, essential when carrying out tracking checks.

Left: An accurate indication of toe-in can now be achieved. The calculation is actually a combination of both front angles that should be within a given limit, to give a toe-in of 0 - 3.18mm (0 - 1/8 in).

Below: Adjustment to the tracking is done by releasing the lock-nut to the track rod end, loosening the steering rack gaiter clip and then rotating the track rod either in or out.

and cleaning them and the inner hub as it's so easy to have a piece of stray debris mess up the sums. The shims can now be added or subtracted as needed and the shaft replaced as soon as possible.

For anyone really after plenty of rear negative and cannot get it by removing shims, more can actually be added between the lower inner fulcrum shaft and the diff. housing. But it really is in a generally inaccessible position and worth doing only if serious modifications are being considered. This is not recommended for everyday use. If you run out of adjustment on the driveshaft, then it might be that you have problems elsewhere.

I had to take the car for a quick blast around the lanes to re-settle things again and then Steve went through the whole lot of measurements once more. Needless to say, something had changed and it had to be at the back, where the driveshaft had to be pulled out and shims dealt with. It worked though and all that remained was the tracking.

Tracking, wheels and tyres

Obviously, with all of the changes we had made, the tracking had altered all by itself. The correct measurement should be 0 - 3.18mm toe in. Steve did this adjustment by releasing the lock-nut on the track rod end and turning the track rod until he achieved the required setting. We were in business. It had taken about half a day to get right but a Jaguar will never

drive like a Jaguar should unless these sensitive settings are correct. Even if you had yours checked a year or so back, then you should have it done again as part of your routine service schedule whether the manufacturer recommends it or not. Remember, tyres will wear at an alarming rate at the slightest sniff of a wrong setting. The car could be potentially dangerous too.

We've decided that we need a new set of wheels and tyres. From a personal level, I want something easier to clean than the original lattice type so we'll be looking around for the best deal.

Acknowledgements:
Bodywork by **The Romford Bodyshop**.
Tel: 01708 723745.
Steering alignment by **Smiley' s Auto Engineers**.
 Tel: 01206 252070.

Next month: Rustproofing.
The all important task of protecting the body work and other vulnerable parts from corrosion.

XJ-S

PROJECT CAR

Part 10: The big freeze. Jim Patten has his air conditioned in our XJ-S

THE STORY SO FAR:

Part 1 (Vol 10 no 4) - *assessment and removing bumpers, front wings, radiator etc.*
Part 2: (Vol 10 no 5) - *engine removal, body jigging, body repairs including inner and outer front wings and front panel.*
Part 3: (Vol 10 no 6) - *panelling up, fitting front wings, bonnet and rear quarter panel.*
Part 4: (Vol 10 no 7) - *rear axle rebuild.*
Part 5: (Vol 10 no 8) - *rear axle rebuild continued.*
Part 6: (Vol 10 no 9) - *front suspension removal and strip.*
Part 7: (Vol 10 no 10) - *top coat, resprayed at last.*
Part 8: (Vol 10 no 11) - *putting the engine back.*
Part 9: (Vol 10 no 12) ^ *steering and suspension alignment*

THE CAR:
XJ-S 3.6 coupe
manufactured 1988,
VIN: SAJJNAEC3CA15441,
purchased as damaged
write-off
December 1997.
Objective: repair, restore,
run and upgrade

I could never quite get the hang of how a refrigerator worked despite the best efforts of our teacher in the science lab. at school. But then a lot of good things slipped me by and a lot of bad lingered. Perhaps that's the way of things. Here we are, years (well, not too many years) down the line and I can't summon up any of those memories to help me understand the workings of the air conditioning in our XJ-S.

It's lucky for us that Eric Henshaw at E H Autos can, he's got the job of re-charging the system. But first, a word about 'old' gases. R12 gas as used on these cars is now illegal. Only licensed users are allowed to work with the system. The equipment they use has non-return, no-escape valves so that none of the R12 gas can escape into the atmosphere. Anyone convicted of allowing these gases to escape would be liable to a £2,500 fine. The latest, 134 gas, is not suitable for this older equipment and converting is just not viable so provided prop-

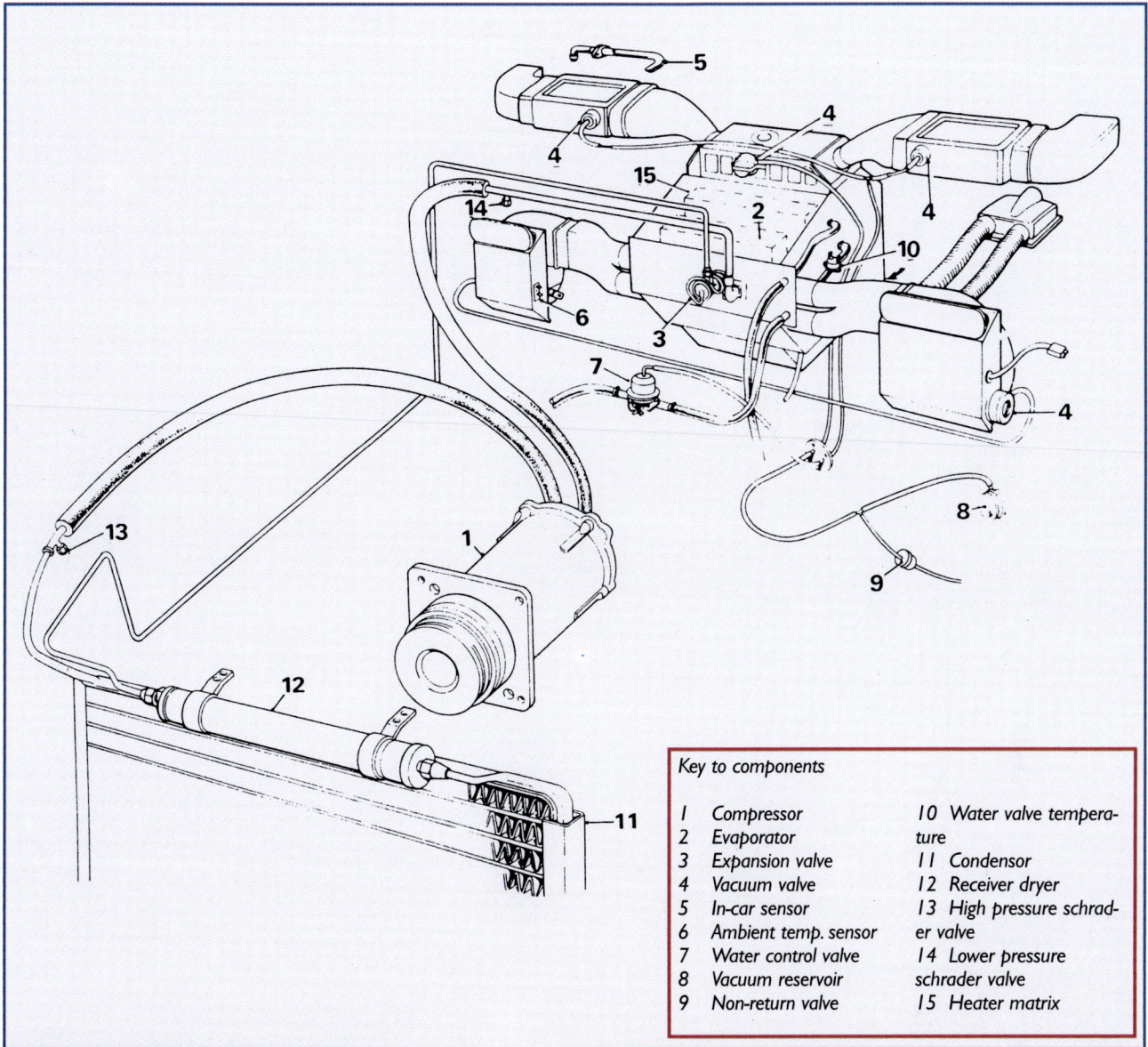

Key to components

1	Compressor	10	Water valve temperature
2	Evaporator		
3	Expansion valve	11	Condensor
4	Vacuum valve	12	Receiver dryer
5	In-car sensor	13	High pressure schrader valve
6	Ambient temp. sensor		
7	Water control valve	14	Lower pressure schrader valve
8	Vacuum reservoir		
9	Non-return valve	15	Heater matrix

2

This piece of kit is absolutely essential for dealing with air conditioning systems.

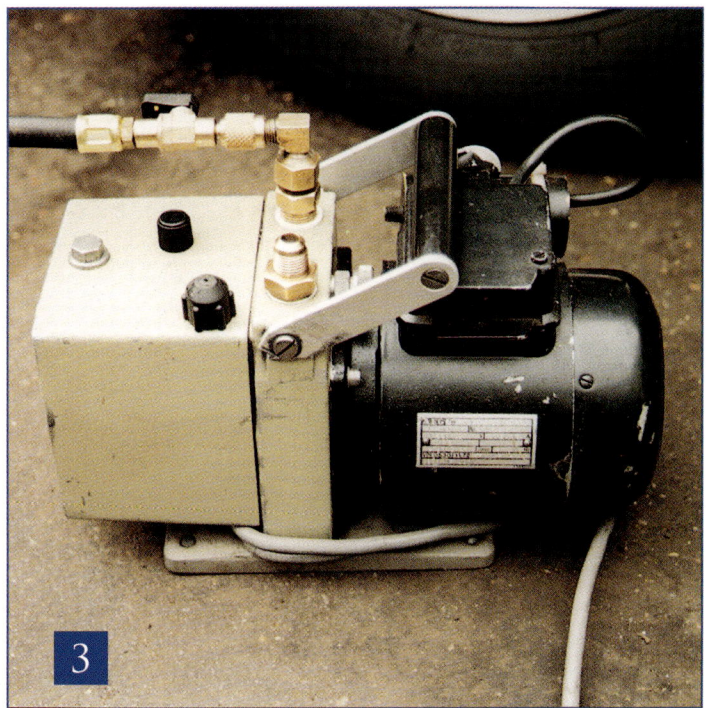

3

Output pipe (attached) delivers evacuated gases safely to a pressure cylinder.

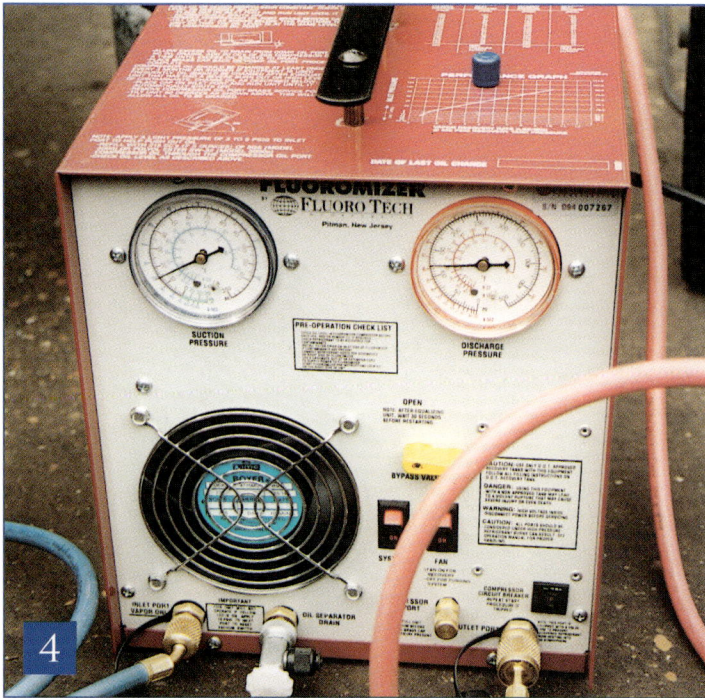

Completely illegal to meddle with unless you are correctly licensed, R12 gases are harmful to the atmosphere.

These pipe ends ensure that minimal loss occurs when the pipe is attached to any part of the system. Pipe colours determine high or low pressure.

Gauges are critical for correct supply. Blue (left) is low pressure with red being high. The centre union deals with evacuated gases.

erly accredited technicians work on the system, it can still be used.

Telling it as it is

Here we have another grand example of not knowing if a system in our car was working or not. I could have run our XJ-S prior to purchase to check out the air conditioning system. The truth is, it didn't even occur to me. We have already replaced the condenser with a unit supplied by David Manners so it was with a great deal of trust that we set about re-charging the system.

What can I say about air conditioning? Well, the system (illustrated) is sealed and uses the outdated R12 gas as mentioned. A compressor (1) running at high pressure draws in low-pressure superheated refrigerant vapour, forcing it around the system where it first meets the condenser (11). This is made of a matrix of finned tubes. The heat is exchanged as air flows through the condenser with the refrigerant vapour travelling inside. The vapour condenses to a cool liquid and, in stages within the condenser, the liquid becomes sub-cooled. In this state, complete condensation has occurred.

Still under pressure, the sub-cooled refrigerant is forced into a receiver/drier (12). This is not only a reservoir for the liquid, it also filters any particles or moisture that may damage the system. Next step for the clean 'dry' liquid is an expansion valve (3) at the inlet to the air conditioning unit. The liquid is metered by the valve, allowing the correct quantity of liquid to an evaporator matrix (2). A capillary senses the temperature and adjusts the valve by closing down to restrict the refrigerant or opens to allow more through.

The evaporator is a low pressure area enabling the refrigerant to suddenly expand as it warms up. At 0.6 degrees C it 'boils' or vaporises . Liquid needs heat to change to vapour and the heat is

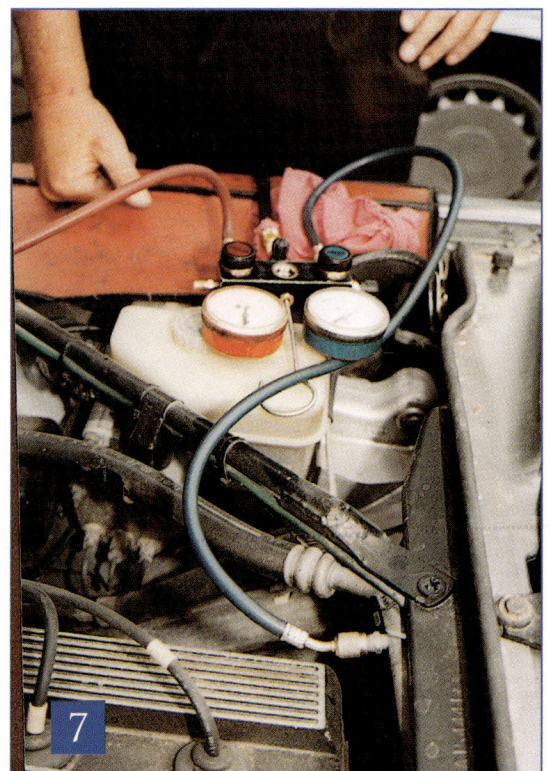

Fresh gases are being delivered through the low pressure pipe on the bulkhead.

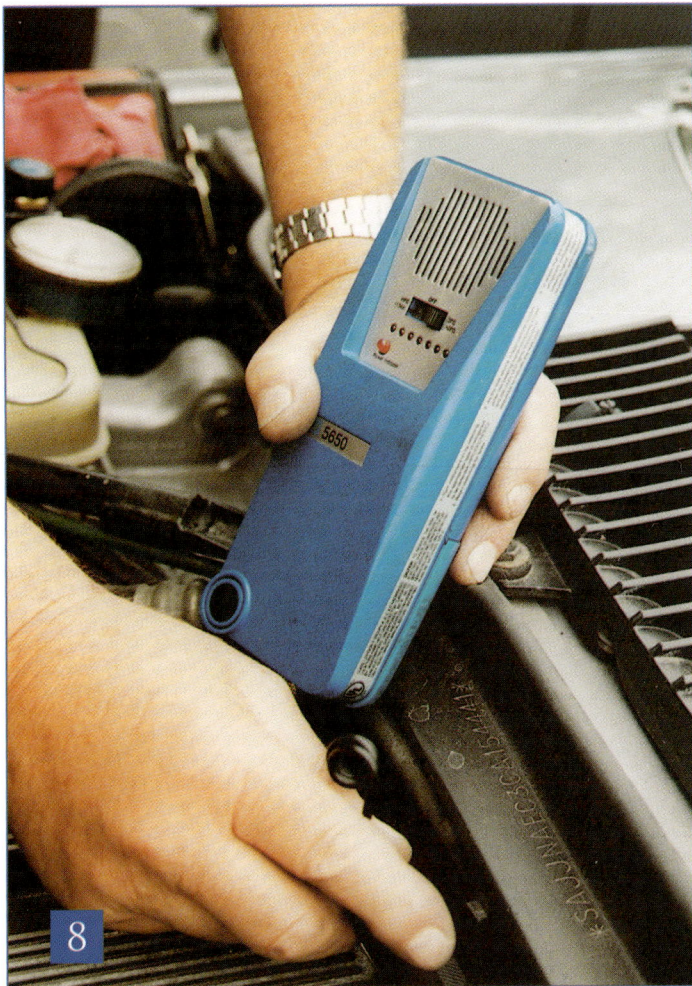

Inspection window on receiver/drier to be used in conjunction with listing. Clear, foamy or bubbles are all good indicators of condition.

Once the system has been charged, an electronic 'sniffer' is run along the pipes to discover any leaks.

taken via the matrix from the interior of the car. Heat transfer continues until the vapour becomes low pressure, superheated vapour. Then it condenses as the whole process starts all over again.

You may have noticed a little pool of water beneath a car with air-conditioning. Well, this happens when the cooled air runs through the evaporator and water vapour in it condenses. The water is drained off through tubes and out beneath the car. Phew! Thank goodness for the workshop manual and the good words received at E H Autos, I would have never got that out on my own. Okay, back to the plot.

It may seem odd but before charging the system it must be evacuated. Although the crash caused an 'interruption' with obvious loss, there will still be refrigerant present. It is also an opportunity to remove excess water from the receiver/drier. Under normal conditions, water is absorbed in the desiccant within the receiver/drier, but the amount is limited. Excess may flow into the expansion valve where it could freeze, effectively stopping the system. Evacuation will take everything with it. But it has do be done correctly without allowing any of the R12 gas into the atmosphere.

A proper recovery machine is needed. It draws the gas from the system, feeds it back into the machine and then pumps it back into a pressurised bottle. The connection from the recovery machine and the valves on the car are by Schrader. In essence, a recovery pipe is connected to the high pressure valve at the front of the engine bay and draws out the old refrigerant through a vacuum. The recovery machine continues running until the gauge reading falls and stabilises. At this point, it continues to operate just to be certain that everything has been extracted from the system. The valves are then shut down, the machine stopped and then

everything is disconnected at the Schrader valve. The system is then ready to be charged.

Charge of the air brigade

This operation must be done immediately after evacuation. The R12 gas is kept in a pressurised cylinder and all connection are of the minimal loss type. This time, charging is made through the low pressure side (near the bulkhead). A high pressure pipe is connected to the high pressure side and then the fresh R12 gas is pumped through the medium of the delivery machine. An exact amount must be delivered - failure to do so would result in a poor system at best or worse, actual damage. Initially between 0.23kg and 0.45kg will be delivered.

Then the high pressure pipe is closed off and the engine started. With an engine speed of 1,500rpm, the air-conditioning blower is set to fast. The flow of refrigerant can be regulated by the suction side of the charging pipe, adding 1.113kg + 0.028kg. The valve is then closed. Another way is to look at the sight glass on the receiver/drier. When the glass clears with no sign of bubbles or foam, the machine is shut off. The engine can then be run for a further five minutes and the sight glass checked again. Slight foaming is permissible, especially if the temperature is below 70 degrees F.

The hoses are then removed from the Schrader valves and the protective sealing caps fitted on the valves. Now it,s time to check every joint connection and the system in general for any leaks. An electronic 'sniffer' is used for this. It will detect the slightest scent of refrigerant (but can be confused if carburettor cleaner has been used). Ours was leak free and what's more, we actually had a fully functioning air conditioning system.

Finally, as a precaution the car doors were left open to air the interior just in case any R12 gas had somehow got into the cabin.

Obviously, with the degree of specialised knowledge and sensitive plant required, this is not a job for just any garage, let alone doing it at home. E H Autos carry out this service regularly. In addition, there are several companies advertising in *Jaguar World* who are experts in this field. The information we have given is purely academic and not intended as an instruction manual on how to do the job (it's not complete enough anyway). It is simply another step in the reconstruction of our accident-damaged car.

Acknowledgements: E H Autos. 01277 631942.

More next month!

XJ-S
PROJECT CAR

In association with
DAVID MANNERS LTD
THE CLASSIC SPECIALIST

Part 11: AJ6 top-end overhaul –
XJ40 owners should be interested in this too. Jim Patten goes off his head.

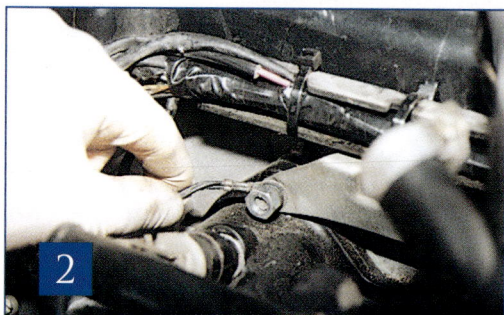

Far left: When releasing the inlet manifold, always note where the earth leads are fitted and make sure that they go back. The engine will never run otherwise.
Left: Rotate the engine to Top Dead Centre (TDC). Just like the XK engine a notch is let into the camshaft to facilitate the use of a TDC tool.

THE STORY SO FAR:

Part 1 (Vol 10 no 4) - assessment and removing bumpers, front wings, radiator etc.
Part 2: (Vol 10 no 5) - engine removal, body jigging, body repairs including inner and outer front wings and front panel.
Part 3: (Vol 10 no 6) - panelling up, fitting front wings, bonnet and rear quarter panel.
Part 4: (Vol 10 no 7) - rear axle rebuild.
Part 5: (Vol 10 no 8) - rear axle rebuild continued.
Part 6: (Vol 10 no 9) - front suspension removal and strip.
Part 7: (Vol 10 no 10) - top coat, resprayed at last.
Part 8: (Vol 10 no 11) - putting the engine back.
Part 9: (Vol 10 no 12) - steering and suspension alignment
Part 10: (Vol 11 no 1) - charging the air conditioning

THE CAR:

XJ-S 3.6 coupe manufactured 1988,
VIN: SAJJNAEC3CA15441,
purchased as damaged write-off December 1997.
Objective: repair, restore, run and upgrade

"Ticks over like an ol' diesel" said a friend climbing into his BMW after listening to our 3.6 coupe. He was right. Our XJ-S had an idle like a London taxicab. Eric Henshaw supplied the reason - a build up of carbon on the valves leading to poor seat sealing at low revs. There was no option: the head had to come off. I arranged to drop the car round to Eric, photograph the dismantling, then push off to Cuba for the Christmas festivities leaving Eric to finish the job while I chased around looking at pre-'59 Yank Tanks.

Removing the cylinder head on the AJ6 engine is a surprisingly straightforward affair. One point to bear in mind, while ordering up the bits, is to remember that the cylinder head bolts are of the stretched type and can be used only once. Order new ones along with your head gasket set.

We would also be converting the car to run on unleaded fuel, the factor here being its lower octane level - valves and seats are up to the job, it's just the ignition timing that needs changing to prevent detonation. It's all quite easy: the sensor bracket on the crankshaft nose is simply changed for the later 4.0 litre type, which effectively alters the timing.

4

With distributor cap and HT leads removed, the single retaining bolt is undone and the distributor lifted out.

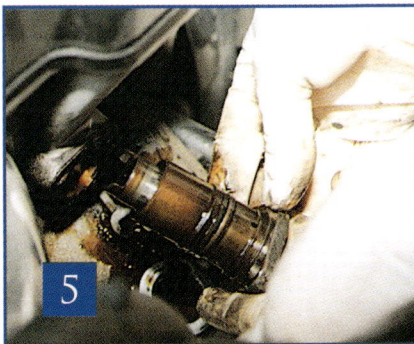

5

The upper timing chain tensioner is held in the side of the head and removed once the retaining bolts have been released.

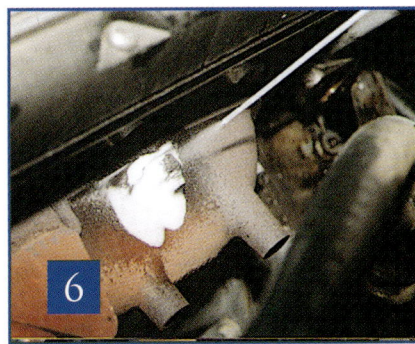

6

Exhaust manifold nuts always rust themselves in place. A good penetrating oil is sprayed on before any attempt to undo them.

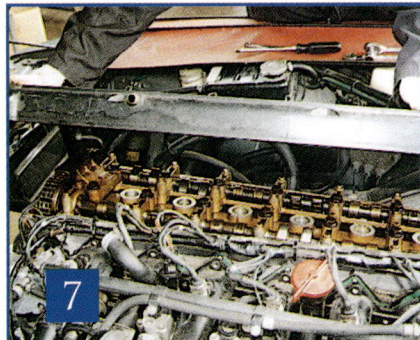

7

The camshaft cover is a one-piece aluminium unit and after removing the retaining nuts, can be lifted away.

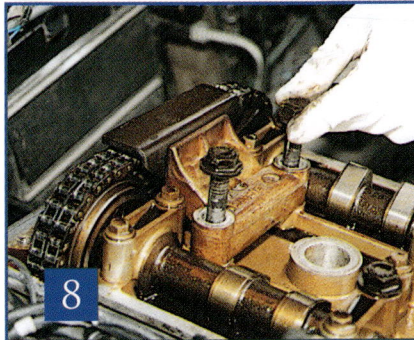

8

A damper/shield is located just above the timing chain and is held in place by a couple of the head bolts. These have to be removed to get access to the chains.

9

The locking wire is cut and removed and the camshaft retaining nuts undone

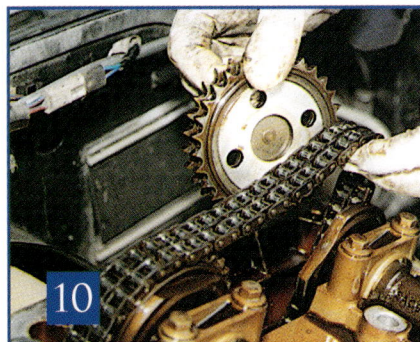

10

Ease off the sprockets from the camshafts and then allow the excess chain to hang over the dampers. An elastic band looped around each damper will stop everything dropping into the engine void.

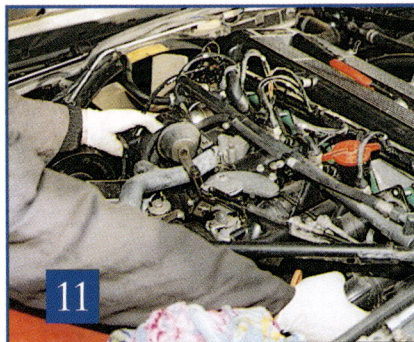

11

Both inlet and exhaust manifolds are eased back from the cylinder head. It may be necessary to either tie them back or enlist a helper to hold them.

12

With everything stripped from the head, all of the retaining bolts can be removed. Remember that these are now redundant as new bolts will be fitted.

13

Two people will be needed to lift the head away but unlike the XK engine, there are no studs to foul on.

14

No appreciable wear was found in the bottom end of the 3.6 litre engine. But then it is noted for its longevity.

15

Quite a build up of carbon was found on the outside of the valves giving warning of what can be found inside.

Note that each camshaft bearing cap is numbered and matches another on the head. No shell bearings are fitted - the camshaft runs in a finely machined cap.

With the caps removed, the camshaft can be lifted away and placed aside.

A magnet us used to lift the tappet buckets out, followed by the shims beneath (the shims often come out with the bucket).

Carbon build-up prevents valve (left) from seating correctly. Compare with new valve (right)

See how the used valve stem seal (right) has expanded compared to a new seal.

With the valves ground in and everything thoroughly cleaned, a check on the valve clearances is made using a conventional feeler gauge. Clearance should be 0.013 inch.

Off with its head.

First, oil and coolant are drained and the oil filter removed. Then, all appendages around the head have to be removed, along with coolant hoses. Although the distributor is not an obstruction in itself, it still has to come out to get access to the lower timing chain tensioner. Like the XK engine, the pistons have to be turned to TDC (top dead centre) position ascertained by a very familiar notch in the camshafts. Again, the camshafts are freed from the timing chain sprockets by cutting the locking wire and removing the securing bolts. To stop the chains falling down inside the engine, lift the excess and lay it over the two dampers. Use a stout elastic band around the dampers to keep everything at rest.

Now, all of the cylinder head bolts can be removed and the head lifted off. Realistically, this is a two-man job as great care must be taken to avoid hitting the open valves. All traces of gasket must be removed from the block and, with all the clutter removed, now is the chance to give this a thorough clean up. Eric Henshaw also gave the head a clean - good practice, and makes working with it that much more pleasant.

Coming apart

Removing the valves is also very similar to XK engine procedure. It's just that there is double the number of valves to take out. I'm glad that Eric's doing this job - my patience wouldn't stand the course.

Each camshaft bearing is numbered to the block for identification. With them all removed, the camshafts could be lifted out and placed aside. The cam buckets are

also similar to those on the XK and are lifted out using a magnet. The valve shims followed in the same way. These were then placed on the bench and the cylinder number noted so that they could be fitted back in the same slot.

Now we were ready to remove the valves - all 24 of them. The XK type valve spring compressor can be used, with a deep recess to get down inside the head. With the flat end on the valve, the other end of the compressor is fitted over the valve end. Before compressing, a slight tap with a small hammer is enough to dislodge the spring retaining cap from the valve stem. Once fully compressed, the valve collets are flipped out and the compressor released. The valve and springs are then collected and placed aside with their position in the head noted. This operation is repeated a further 23 times...

Valve stem seals are fitted on the inlet side. These harden and allow oil to be drawn past the seal and into the cylinder. That's when you see puffs of blue smoke from the exhausts of the odd XJ-S or XJ40.

At last we could see what all the fuss was about. There was certainly a huge amount of carbon build-up down the valve stems. On a couple of them it was so severe that the valve could not seat correctly. Eric examined each valve and his assessment was that they would all 'go again' after they had been cleaned of carbon.

Easier said than done but Eric has been at this Jaguar game for some time. He was able to put each valve in the chuck of the lathe (a quality electric drill with perfect head bearings would do) and clean the carbon away with either a proper scraper, or various grades of abrasive paper. It's okay to use coarse on the carbon alone. Never use it on the valve stem or severe

damage will result.

Each valve and seat was given a light cut to clean the surface ready for grinding in. Do not underestimate the time this operation takes. It could run into a couple of days to do all 24.

First, course valve grinding paste is applied to the seat and valve face. Then, using a valve grinding stick, the valve is rotated back and forth with the paste acting between the seat and face. As soon as a uniform grey appearance has been achieved all of the way around seat and face, all traces of coarse paste are removed and the procedure repeated using fine. When a vicar's collar of light grey is seen on both surfaces, that's it and the next valve can be tackled.

With all valves ground in, every trace of paste must be removed otherwise it could penetrate into the engine and carry on grinding where it's not wanted. Well, just writing it has tired me out - what must it be like to actually do it?

Re-fitting the valves is a reversal of the removal procedure, but using new valve springs. A copious amount of oil is used to pre-lubricate, especially around the camshaft bearing caps. The camshafts are rotated (with the other not fully tightened down) to settle down.

Time now for some simple arithmetic. It,s quite likely that all valve clearances will have changed despite putting the original valve shims back in their right places. Once again, the system for obtaining clearance is the same as the XK engine. Valve clearances are 0.012 to 0.14in. Measure each gap with the lobe of the cam in the fully upright position. Then the calculations are taken. If the clearance is

These timing chain dampers were in pretty poor shape and would need changing. That requires removal of the timing chain cover.

The large nut on the crankshaft damper is removed and the damper tapped off using a soft face mallet.

With all timing chain cover nuts removed, the soft face mallet is used again to dislodge the timing chain cover.

Now the timing chain assembly could be dismantled followed by the timing chain guide/dampers.

This is the bracket holding the electronic timing sensor. To obtain the correct timing, a 4.0 litre bracket is used

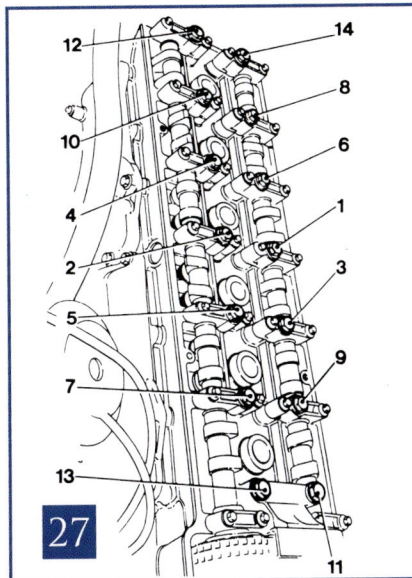

Ensure that the correct sequence is used when tightening the cylinder head. Tighten to a torque of 38-40ib/ft and the bolts are turned exactly 90 degrees

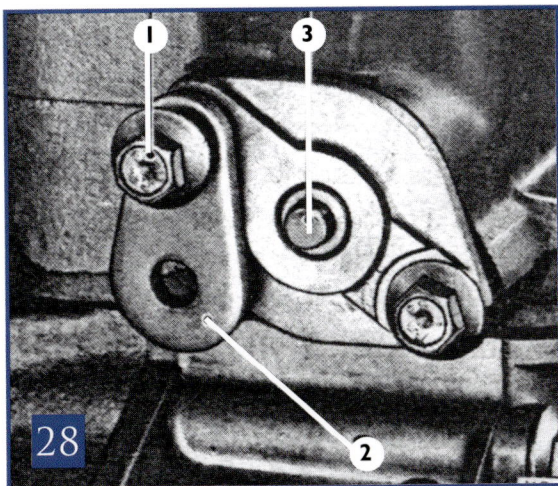

When re-assembling the timing chains, it is essential that everything be done at TDC. If the existing top chain tensioner is being used, the 'O' ring must be replaced, lubricated with oil. Turn the valve retainer securing bolt (1) four complete turns. The tensioner is released using a 3mm Allen key, turned anti-clockwise. Then fit the valve assembly (2) and engage the retainer plate (3) before fully tightening the securing bolt.

say 0.010 in. with a shim measuring 0.100 the formula is as follows. Shim size plus clearance minus correct gap. 0.100 + 0.010 - 0.013 = 0.097. So a shim size of 0.097 will be needed.

Jaguar identify shims alphabetically, A being 0.085in and going up to X at 0.108in. Sometimes it is possible to swap shims around using whatever is in the engine but many still have to be bought. Always double check the measurements and don't be surprised if after carefully completing the job, some clearances are out. There's no real explanation, it just happens.

A damper on the proceedings.

It took time of course but soon the head was ready to fit. Except that the timing chain dampers were thoroughly thrashed. So we went the whole way and fitted new damper guides and timing chains. It all sounds very straightforward but in reality took quite a bit of time. I never witnessed what went on (my yearly sunshine fix) but I think I grasped the following correctly from Eric and the workshop manual.

First the radiator fan and housing had to be removed, then the crankshaft pulley along with the ignition sensor (as mentioned, we were replacing the bracket anyway to convert over to unleaded fuel). Next came the timing chain cover, a simple matter of securing nuts.

Extracting the seal/crankshaft damper spacer proved a nightmare. Eric spent an age trying to drive this obstinate part away from the crankshaft. A new spacer came with the oil seal so damage was of no importance. All chains were then removed along with the damaged dampers. David Manners had sent suitable replacements through (all correct) enabling Eric to start boxing the car up again.

I am told that re-assembly was quite uneventful. The cylinder head was re-fitted with a new gasket along with new bolts. It was tightened to a torque of 38 - 40 lb/ft. The bolt is then turned through exactly 90 degrees. This I know sets the nerves on edge but it has to be done. It is essential that the correct tightening sequence (see diagram) be observed.

With everything assembled, and new oil and coolant added, the car fired first time. It was then coupled up to the Gas Analyzer for adjustment. It was all going so well when suddenly, engine revs rose by 500rpm and the readings went wild...

We reveal all next month.

Thanks to EH Autos 01277 631942

XJ-S
PROJECT CAR

In association with
DAVID MANNERS LTD
THE CLASSIC SPECIALIST

Part 12: Current Conundrums. Sparks fly as Jim Patten is stranded.

THE STORY SO FAR:

Part 1: (Vol 10 no 4) - assessment and removing bumpers, front wings, radiator etc.
Part 2: (Vol 10 no 5) - engine removal, body jigging, body repairs including inner and outer front wings and front panel.
Part 3: (Vol 10 no 6) - panelling up, fitting front wings, bonnet and rear quarter panel.
Part 4: (Vol 10 no 7) - rear axle rebuild.
Part 5: (Vol 10 no 8) - rear axle rebuild continued.
Part 6: (Vol 10 no 9) - front suspension removal and strip.
Part 7: (Vol 10 no 10) - top coat, resprayed at last.
Part 8: (Vol 10 no 11) - putting the engine back.
Part 9: (Vol 10 no 12) ^ steering and suspension alignment
Part 10: (Vol 11 no 1) charging the air conditioning
Part 11: (Vol 11 no 2) cylinder head decarbonising

THE CAR:
XJ-S 3.6 coupe
manufactured 1988,
VIN:
SAJJNAEC3CA15441,
purchased as damaged
write-off
December 1997.
Objective: repair,
restore,
run and upgrade

"Emergency - I've got a flashing FF5 going over to FF6. I don't think I can hold it much longer, Jim."

"Engineering, divert power from the main thrusters, isolate the lithium crystals and feed everything you have to the warp drive engines."

"Wow, it worked, we've just avoided being sucked through an inter-space jump gate. Good thinking bridge. Over and out."

Power Down

Oh, that we had access to the Star Ship Enterprise engineering team. It seems that we have some electrical problems that are proving difficult to track down. After a successful decarbonisation of the cylinder head, our XJ-S ran as sweetly as a car could. But when it was coupled up to the diagnostic machine, the readings went all over the place and we knew we were in trouble. The computer flashed FF5 which trans-

lates to 'airflow meter high throttle potentiometer low incompatible'. Next time it flashed FF6, a change of attitude this time to 'airflow meter low throttle potentiometer high incompatible'. Yes - our electronic helpmate was in fact selling us a load of tosh!

We haven't got Geordie of the Federation, but we do have the next best, Eric Henshaw at E H Autos. Eric set to work on his usual routine. It was fairly obvious at this stage that the throttle potentiometer needed an interview. There's no real way of testing so we tried a new unit. No change. We could dismiss the airflow

meter as this too had been replaced earlier by an AJ6 modified unit (more on that later) and this had been fully bench tested by Roger Bywater before despatch. Eric has experienced a flood of problems with Jaguar fuel injection harness lately, firstly on V12 cars but more recently, AJ6-engined cars too.

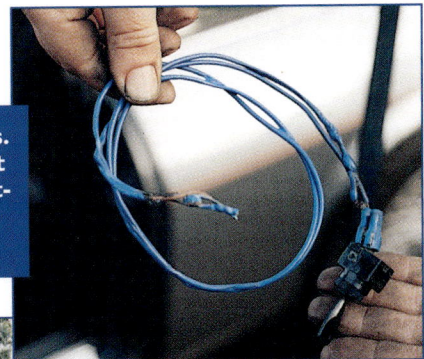

What appears to happen is that engine heat causes the harness to become brittle. In severe cases the loom actually breaks up. A continuity test along each wire has drawn a blank but then it has before. It's

Our dead XJ-S heads off on John Harris' transporter to E H Autos for some remedial work.

The original Jaguar radio is held in position with rivets. These have to be drilled out to facilitate removal.

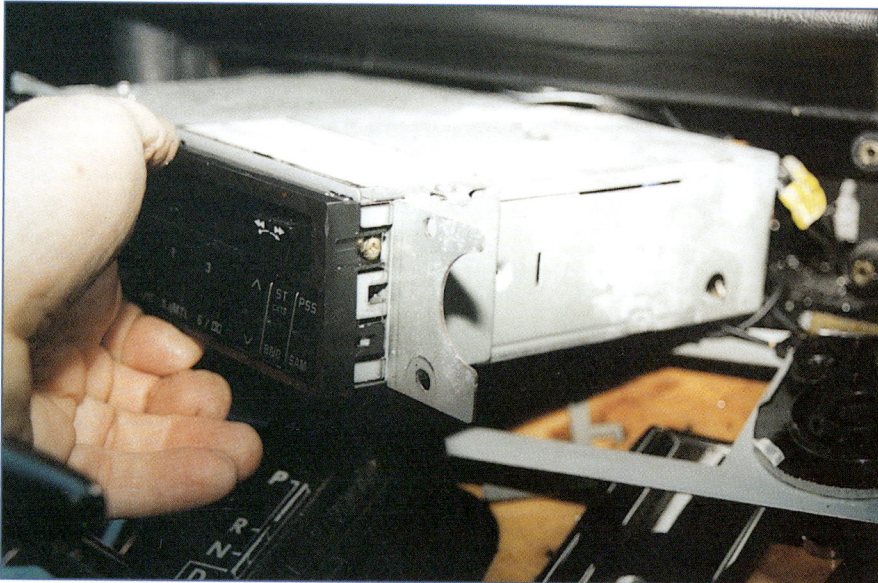

Nothing else holds the radio in place and it can be pulled out of the aperture.

This may look a nightmare of coloured spaghetti but it does all make sense once everything has been identified. Tags label all wires.

almost as though the wire casing is breaking down not sufficiently enough to cause a short but enough to allow some sort of magnetic interaction between closely juxtaposed wires. This would most certainly explain our conflicting signals. We decided to bite the bullet and order a new harness - except it has just gone NLA, the dreaded letters which mean No Longer Available!

Jaguar have apparently had so little demand for this part that it was deemed not worth keeping in stock. However, some faults have a habit of showing themselves only when age sets in. At the moment, even with all our contacts we have no answer and at the time of writing our XJ-S is VOR - another chilling term, this one industry parlance for Vehicle Off Road.

Ours is not a unique situation. We've heard of other owners who have suffered similar experiences.

But we decided to turn a negative into a positive (to use an apt electrical simile!). We know these problems are occurring and we would like to investigate ways of solving them. However, specialists cannot hope to provide a solution unless there is a demand. Write to us and tell us of your difficulties and we will do our best to negotiate a cure. Or better still, if you are in the business and have come across these situations and have the answer, then contact us: you could suddenly expand your order book. So hopefully more on this next month.

Now let's rewind the clock a little. Prior to the decoke, a hiccup occurred in the form of a breakdown. No warning, no symptoms, the car just shut down shortly after starting one morning. I had no answer so threw it over to Eric. And that meant calling in John Harris and his transporter (John owns an E-type and is used to moving our sort of cars).

Eric worked methodically through the car but was getting a bit bogged down. Then by chance he found it. A blue wire was spotted under the dash. It shouldn't have been there. Following the wire through he found that it changed from being a regular shape to a molten mess. The end was crudely patched into the impact isolation switch. This device is built in to the car so that in the event of a collision the switch is thrown and fuel supply cut off. Some previous owner, in an effort to install an anti-theft device, had plumbed another switch into this system.

Now this sort of thing is okay on

The new radio/cassette is slightly bigger than the old so the aperture is ever so slightly enlarged with a file.

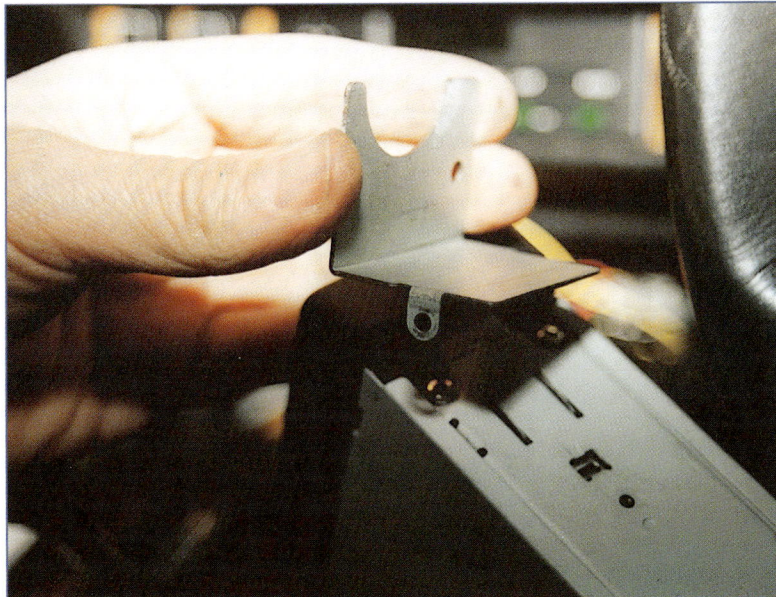

Side retaining brackets from the Jaguar radio are transferred over to our new set.

All new wires are connected to each individual feed and then the multi-plug fits into the back of the radio/cassette.

a car of simple design. I did it myself at college with a Mini. A switch hidden beneath the back seat wired in to the electric fuel pump meant that when I left the car, the fuel supply could be cut off. But a Mini has a very basic wiring harness. An XJ-S does not and its electronics rejected this foreign object but in doing so, wires melted with obvious consequences. Luckily, the damage had not gone any further. Once Eric had removed the bodge we were back in business.

Wot, no music?

The XJ-S is a car for classical music. Pavarotti gave his all and the XJ-S loved it. Then I had a change of mood. A bit of blues and Stevie Ray Vaughan. Just as I was getting into it, the XJ-S decided enough, chewed up the tape and swallowed it. I was devastated! How could I trust the tape machine again? A quick call to John Lane at Motorways Autostore paid off. John had a small stock of Jensen radio cassettes. With a maximum output of 45W per channel, it should be enough to deal with my varied music taste.

Removing the failed unit was easy enough except that I discovered that it was riveted in. With a domestic drill, I removed the rivets and then used a vacuum to clean up the swarf. That allowed me to remove the original radio/cassette. The wires were disconnected from a multi-plug but of course, this was different from the new unit. However, the instructions were easy to follow and all the original wiring was clearly marked so I didn't need my union card to complete the job.

Great! It handled ZZ Top with ease. But I haven't been able to use the car since my visit to Cuba and I've a pile of Cuban Salsa to try out. Can't wait.

Acknowledgements.
E H Autos: 01277 631942
Vehicle Transportation. John Harris:
0836 232114
Motorways Autostore:
0181 592 0294

Fully installed the new radio/cassette is ready to entertain.

XJ-S PROJECT CAR

Part 13: Jim Patten avoids looming disaster as the wiring fault is found. A new water pump cures a dribble and a replacement supply pipe stops the auto box leaking.

THE STORY SO FAR:

Part 1 (Vol 10 No 4) assessment and removing bumpers, front wings. Radiator etc.

Part 2: (VOl 10 No 5) engine removal, body jigging, body repairs including inner and outer front wings and front panel.

Part 3: (Vol 10 No 6) - panelling up, fitting front wings, bonnet and rear quarter panel. Part 4: (Vol 10 No 7) rear axle rebuild.

Part 5: (Vol 10 No 8) rear axle rebuild continued.

Part 6: (Vol 10 No 9) front suspension removal and strip.

Part 7: (Vol 10 No 10) top coat, resprayed at last.

Part 8: (Vol 10 No 11) putting the engine back.

Part 9: (Vol 10 No 12) steering alignment.

Part 10: (Vol 11 No 1) charging the air conditioning.

Part 11: (Vol 11 No 2) cylinder head de-carbonising.

Part 12: (Vol 11 No 3) wiring problems and new radio/cassette.

THE CAR

XJS 3.6 Coupe manufactured 1988,
VIN: SAJJNAEC3CA15441,
purchased as damaged write-off December 1997.
Objective: repair, restore, run and upgrade.

ERIC Henshaw at E H Autos reckons this past six months has been a torrid time for Jaguar wiring. He has fitted more engine looms in that period than in the whole of his business life. Others are saying the same sort of thing. But now, the engine loom is no longer available from Jaguar, so other avenues have to be explored. Eric has carried out every single continuity test imaginable, but the readings kept coming up as correct. Our car had other ideas though as still the Fuel Fail reading was showing.

Harnessing the power

THERE was only one option left - remove and dismantle the loom. First Eric had to unclip it from the ECU situated in the passenger footwell. After first undoing a couple of securing bolts, the ECU was free and the harness was pulled clear. It also needs to be disconnected from a couple of relays too. The loom is very tight as it runs through the plenum into the engine bay. It's necessary to release the four nuts holding the plate over the plenum and slipping off the rubber waterproof boot. Once the loom has been eased through into the engine bay, it's just a matter of following it through, releasing the various multi-connectors and extracting it from the torturous route it takes. It's a good idea to make sketches or take photographs to make sure that everything goes back as it came out.

Eric then unwound the loom casing and some surprises came to light. A resistor that is linked in to the throttle potentiometer was found to be faulty and a wire running to the air flow meter had started to burn through its casing. This was probably caused by another section traced back to the bulkhead where the casing was chafing on a sharp edge. The following photographs give an overview of the procedure but unless you're qualified in these matters, it's suggested that you seek specialist help.

1 This wire has started to burn through the outer casing, exposing its wires. It supplies the air flow meter.

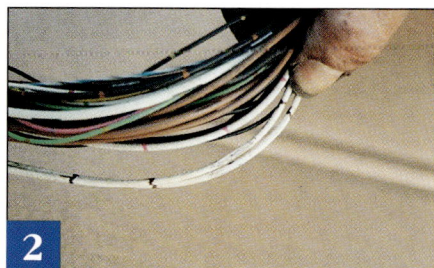

2 More evidence of chafing against a raw edge was found further back in the air flow meter wire. It would be padded upon re-assembly.

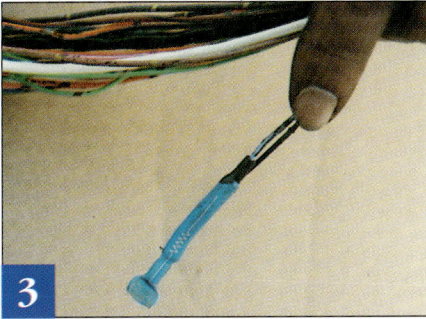

3 This resistor had given up all resistance and was replaced. It's actually bound into the loom, making location difficult.

4 The harness passes through the bulkhead at this point where a rubber boot keeps out the elements.

5 It's a tight area beneath this cover plate and the plenum below. Removing the bolts gives access to the routing.

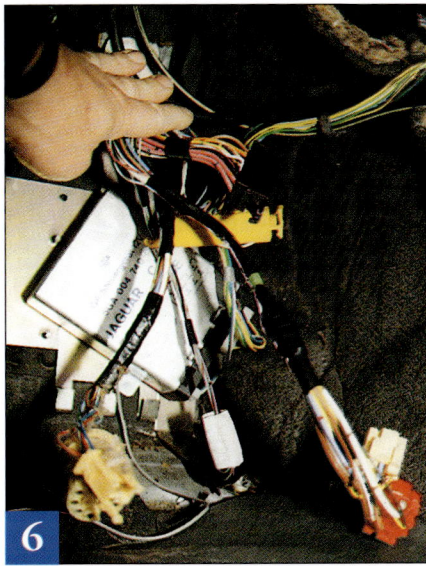

6 Here, the repaired loom is being passed into the footwell. It really is difficult to get the whole lot through.

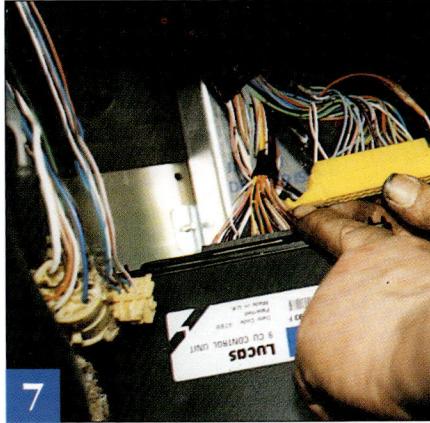

7 To connect up to the ECU, the multi block has to be clipped in and then eased down on to the connections.

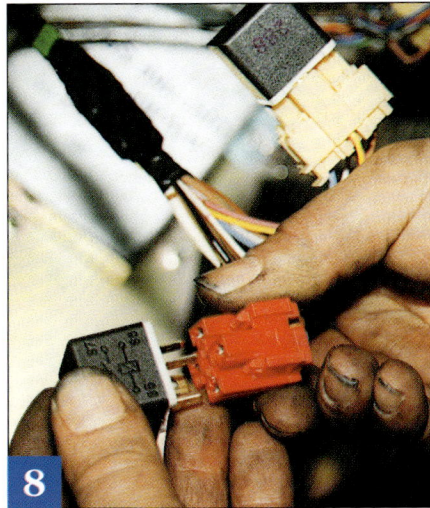

8 Relays fit to their respective plugs. The pattern of the spade connectors dictate what goes where.

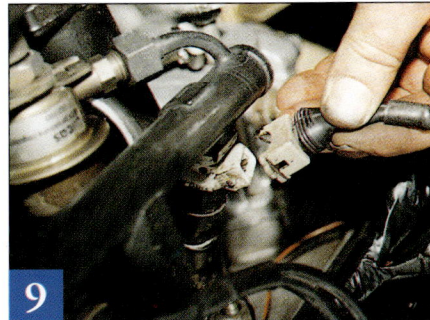

9 Working back inside the engine bay, all six connectors are fitted to the fuel injection rail.

10 It's essential that all earth connections are replaced otherwise all sorts of faults will be thrown up.

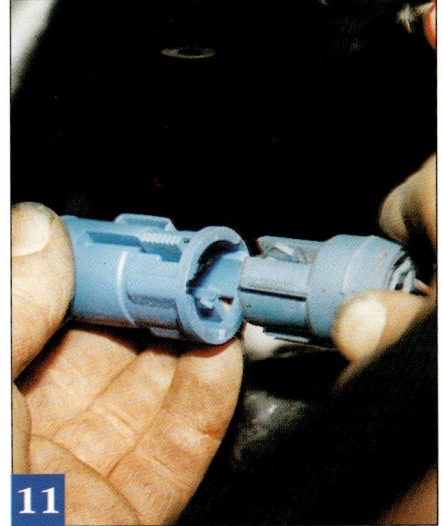

11 Most multi-connectors are unique to each other and are colour coded. For instance, this one is blue and the plug will not fit any other.

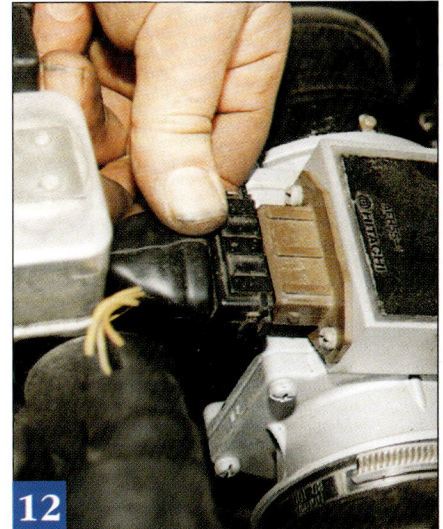

12 Other connections are obvious. The section to the air flow meter falls naturally into place and the plugs again, are unique.

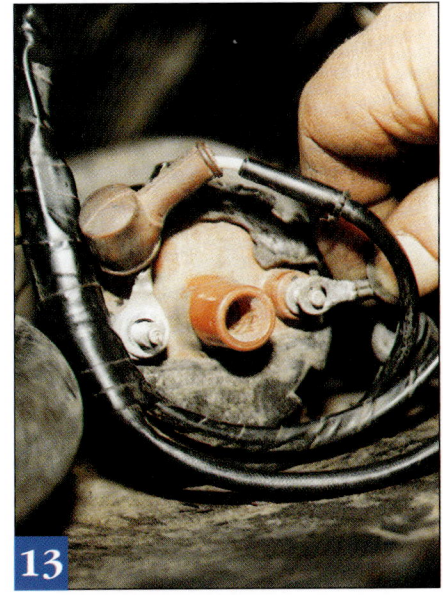

13 Coil connections are easy too as the ring connectors are of different sizes making wrong footing almost impossible.

Auto gearbox oil cooler supply pipe

OUR XJS had started to dribble. One trace was oil, the other water. These were eventually traced to one of the automatic gearbox oil cooler supply pipes and the water was actually coming from the pump itself.

We started with the oil pipe. Looked simple enough. Just undo one end at the radiator followed by one at the gearbox. That's until the route the pipe takes is spotted. From radiator it dives alongside the engine block, slips beneath the steering rack and then takes a trip over the auto box to arrive at the other side. It would mean removing the gearbox mount and lowering the gearbox to get access. At least the pipe was pre-shaped, but it cost almost £100! The pictures will show where the pipe runs.

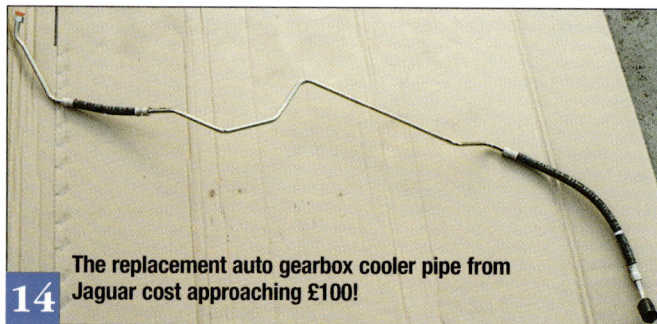

14 The replacement auto gearbox cooler pipe from Jaguar cost approaching £100!

15 Its route starts at the radiator. See how damp the pipe is. It is actually leaking from the crimped joint, a fairly common problem.

16 Although out of vision, the cooler pipe takes a run nearby the power steering rack.

17 Once the pipe gets near the gearbox, it climbs over the top before dropping down the other side where it connects to the 'box.

Plugging the leak

ALTHOUGH the water pump was working OK, water was streaming out near the pulley seal. Replacement was fairly straightforward. Just three bolts hold it to the engine where the various coolant pipes join.

Removal entails extracting the fan cowl and viscous fan. Then all pipes are disconnected before undoing the three retaining bolts. The pump is lifted out and the new one installed. No gaskets are involved but the opportunity should be taken to examine all hoses and clips. More pictures show how the job was done.

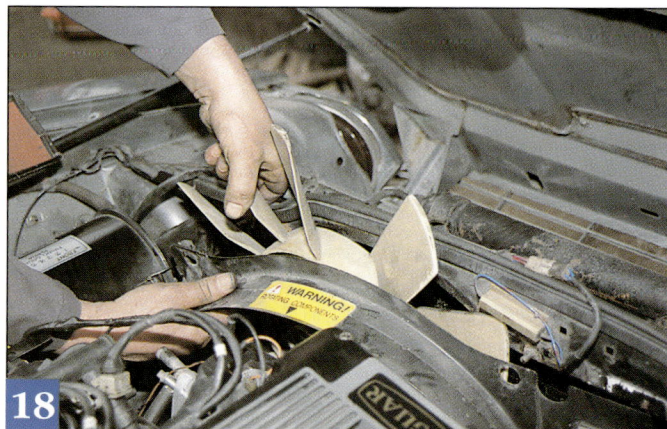

18 To get access to the water pump, first the cooling cowl has to be loosened and then the viscous fan removed. Always check the fan bearings, ours were OK.

19 Here, the pump is seen still attached to the engine block with a couple of pipes already removed.

20 With all pipes removed, the three securing bolts can be extracted.

21 These are the bolts holding the pump to the block. Note that one is shorter than the other two. This enables it to slip in beneath the pulley.

22 The pump can now be removed from the car. Access is easy and extraction no problem.

23 Note the leak from a failed seal near to the pulley.

24 The studs holding the viscous fan have to be swapped over. If a stud extractor is not available, two nuts locked together will serve just as well.

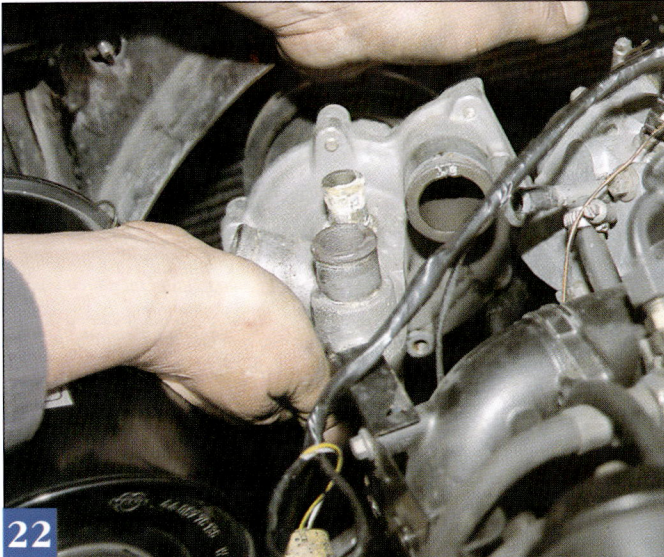

25 Fitting the bolts before offering the pump back into the car makes re-assembly easier.

26 The pump is refitted in a reversal of the removal procedure.

Our thanks go to E H Autos. Tel: 01277 631942.

Next month: **Rustproofing (at last!)**

XJ-S PROJECT CAR

In association with

DAVID MANNERS LTD
THE CLASSIC SPECIALIST

Part 14: At last, Jim Patten covers the rust proofing of our XJ-S.

THE CAR
XJ S 3.6 Coupe manufactured 1988,
VIN: SAJJNAEC3CA15441,
purchased as damaged write-off December 1997.
Objective: repair, restore, run and upgrade.

It would appear that rust proofing features have become *Jaguar World's* red buses. Nothing for ages and then two come along together. Well, it made sense to cover both the XK150 and XJ-S as the equipment was on hand with 50% of the *JW* editors having some enthusiasm for the sport. Paul Skilleter finds the process relaxing and gains a considerable sense of achievement knowing that he has given another car protection for the future.

I, on the other hand, hate the prospect of laying on my back getting smothered in wax. Whilst I fully appreciate the sentiments and go along with the reasoning, I'd prefer if others did the work for me. And that's where Paul Roach comes into the picture. He was landed with the XJ-S, Paul Skilleter did the XK 150.

Well equipped

EVERYONE has their own idea about how to go about rust proofing but really there is only one way to go, and that is with all guns blazing with plenty of pressure.

I use a Sealey wax injector gun that

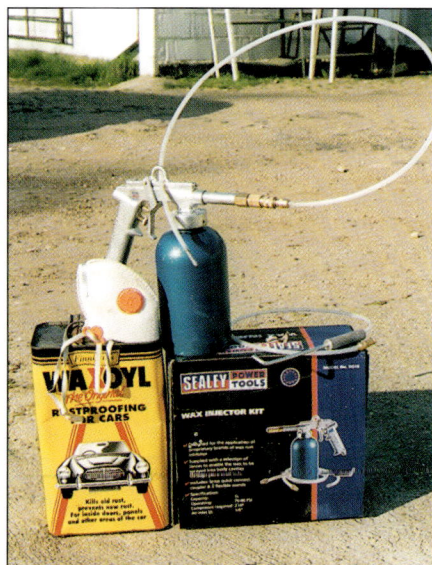

Tools of the trade. Waxoyl, a face mask and the Sealey wax injector kit.

operates from a compressor operating at between 70-80 psi. At this sort of pressure, the wax is forced into every panel. There can be no hiding place.

Extension wands with different nozzles allow access to virtually any section. Small, hand prime applicators are okay for gentle applications but when a full blown job is required, there can be no compromise.

There are many rustproofing products on the market and few are actually bad. I've always used Waxoyl and although I cannot say that I've carried out any scientific tests, I can say that my cars are used in all conditions and have yet to see any deterioration.

Paul Skilleter will tell you of his favoured product elsewhere. Waxoyl in its as-bought state is too thick to pass through the gun and so a thinning process is required.

White spirit works well if conditions are cold. In warmer atmosphere, keeping the can in a bucket of hot water naturally thins the wax. High ambient temperatures keep the fluidity at a reasonable level. In cold, the wax hardens up too quickly and that's where the white spirit proves its worth. Although Waxoyl is perfectly safe, wearing a protective mask is recommended.

1

2

Another hole has been drilled into the sill end panel. Using a long probe, the wand is pushed down the length of the sill and pulled back while operating the gun. The multi-directional nozzle ensures that total coverage is achieved. The radius arm mount box section was treated next and 8mm grommets used to seal the hole.

See how excess Waxoyl pours out of the drain channels. Keeping these channels clear should be part of any bodywork service routine.

3

Left: Beneath the rear wheel arch: A hole is drilled into the radius arm mount box section.

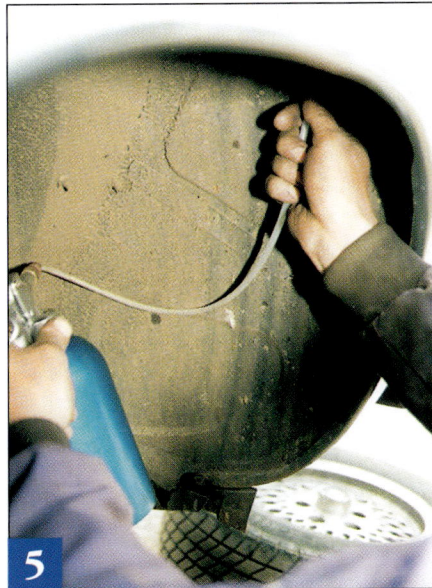

4

Left: More holes are drilled in the chassis legs over the rear axle cage. One at the top and another each side complete the area.

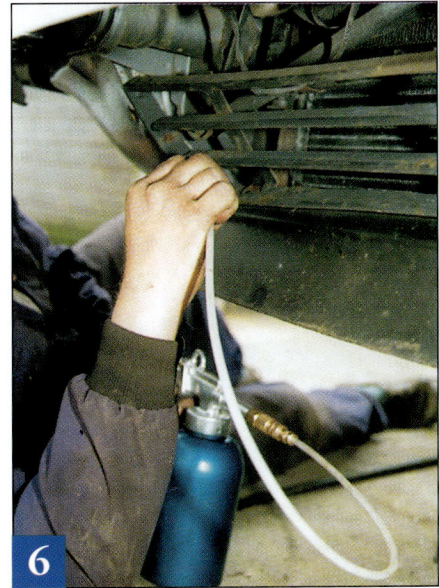

5

It is possible to remove the entire front splash panel and get directly into the nose section but we prefer to drill an access hole and saturate the area.

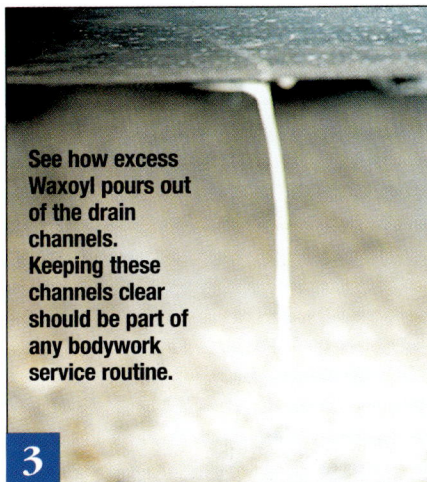

6

A cross-member runs beneath the radiator and it is very difficult to get at. Keep at it because this section is very vulnerable to rust. The outside is given a dousing too.

7

We mentioned in an earlier episode how the box sections beneath the front wings rot. It is essential that they are treated. Three grommets are already fitted and give easy access.

A power drill with an 8mm bit is needed to get access to hidden box sections. Always fit a grommet after drilling any holes. One of the easiest ways to determine where to apply the treatment is to go have a look at a rusted version of your car. Check out the bad spots and make sure that yours is covered there. Better still, rustproof wherever you can.

What a mess!

SHORT of tipping an automatic gearbox up on end and swinging it around the garage, rustproofing is the messiest job you will ever do on your car. So be prepared.

The best way is to minimise the unsightly mess is to use a huge plastic sheet, mount the car above it and then simply roll it up at the end of the day.

If the car has been used on the road then there will be an accumulation of road dirt to deal with. Try a wire brush if you will but the only sure way is the use of a power or jet wash. I usually jet wash the underside and then either pop the car inside a Carcoon or leave it in the garage with a de-humidifier running. Failing that, take it for a 30 mile run. This will remove all traces of water.

The car will now be in a suitable state to rustproof. Follow the pictures for an insight into how we treated our XJ-S.

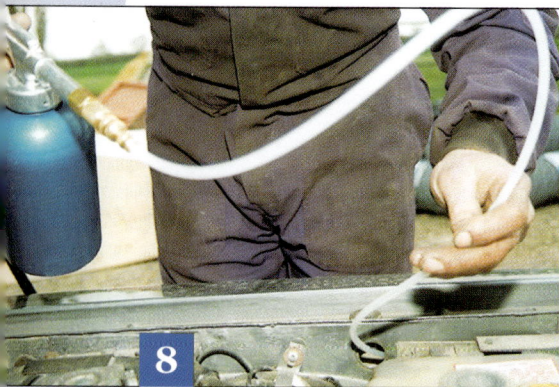

8

The flexible extension is used to get into the full length of the box section. Waxoyl mist could be seen escaping from every aperture.

11

A bit of surface rust was evident around the bonnet seams and so extensive coverage was applied to the outer surface of the affected areas.

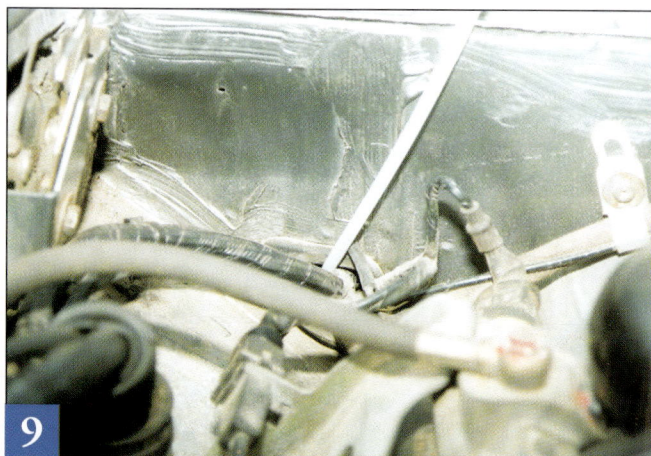

9

Use every opportunity. In the far corner of the engine bay near to the bulkhead, the wiring loom passes through a grommet. It is possible to push the applicator through and give the back of the wing/sill top a good dowsing.

12

We had already treated the insides of the doors when the casings were off, but it is possible to carry out similar protection by pushing the nozzle into the door shell behind the door casing.

Bonnets suffer from rot but there are many access points. We entered each and gave a good blast of wax to fully treat the inner shell.

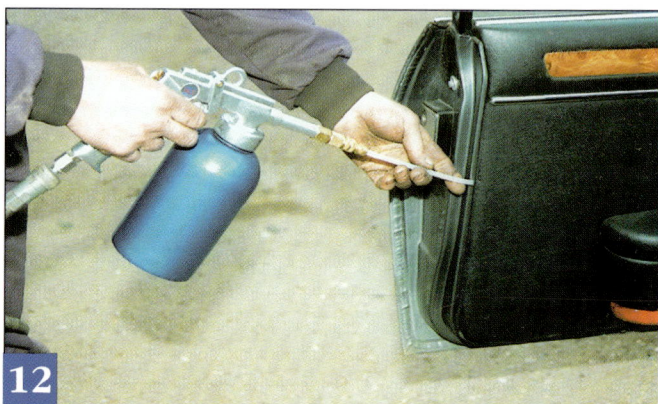

10

Boot-lids rust badly so it pays to protect them using the many access holes already present. If Paul Roach looks a bit bleary eyed, have sympathy. Wife Julie had just delivered their first child, a daughter called Bethany. Well done you two.

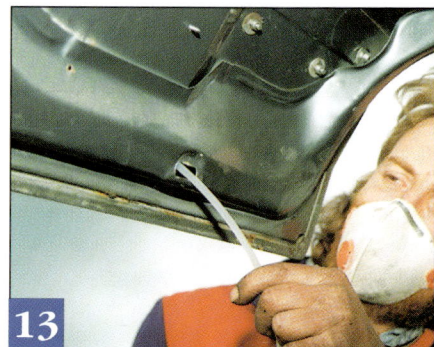

13

PAUL carried on checking all seams and looked for breaks in the existing underbody sealant. We chose not to apply another coating over Jaguar's original sealant, although we could have generally sprayed black Waxoyl over the entire underside. Had we just finished a complete back to metal restoration then we would have done things differently.

No matter how hard you try, the smell of Waxoyl will linger inside the cabin of the car. We left it outside with the windows wound down in a futile effort to air the interior. My drive back was also with the windows down hoping that the draught would help. It did to an extent, but time alone will really cure the pong.

We're just about done with the XJ-S. Just a good clean up and wheels and tyres to sort out. As a project it has certainly been interesting.

We never started with the intention of showing how to buy an accident damaged car and put it back on the road economically. The aim was to show that just because a car has been bent, proper repairs are just as valid as for any restoration. I am often surprised at various reactions. There are those who are quite happy to braze up an old car in the garage and put a ghastly lash-up on the road and yet will throw up their hands in disgust at the thought of an accident damaged repaired car. Such strange attitudes.

There were many other aspects of this car that apply to all XJ-S variants. Suspension and brake rebuilds. The electrical difficulties we encountered and the cylinder head overhaul are relevant to many owners.

Working with David Manners has been a good experience too and we were pleased with the quality of the service and the parts we received. It takes a brave company to gear up for a car that had yet to gain popularity. Yet that is the position David Manners took when the XJ-S was just another old Jaguar. Enthusiasts have a lot to thank for his foresight.

It's not over yet.

Next month

We fit our wheels and new tyres and report back on how our XJ-S performs on the road. Then we will be looking for a new owner.

XJ-S PROJECT CAR

In association with

DAVID MANNERS LTD
THE CLASSIC SPECIALIST

Part 15: Conclusion! Jim Patten fits a big-bore throttle, new wheels and tyres and gives his personal views on living with our XJ-S

THE STORY SO FAR:

Part 1 (Vol 10 no 4) assessment and removing bumpers, front wings. Radiator etc.
Part 2: (VOl 10 no 5) engine removal, body jigging, body repairs including inner and outer front wings and front panel.
Part 3: (Vol 10 no 6) - panelling up, fitting front wings, bonnet and rear quarter panel. Part 4: (Vol 10 no 7) rear axle rebuild.
Part 5: (Vol 10 no 8) rear axle rebuild continued.
Part 6: (Vol 10 no 9) front suspension removal and strip.
Part 7: (Vol 10 no 10) top coat, resprayed at last.
Part 8: (Vol 10 no 11) putting the engine back.
Part 9: (Vol 10 no 12) steering alignment.
Part 10: (Vol 11 no 1) charging the air conditioning.
Part 11: (Vol 11 no 2) cylinder head decarbonising.
Part 12: (Vol 11 no 3) wiring problems and new radio/cassette.
Part 13: (Vol 11 no 4) wiring resolved, auto gearbox pipe replaced.
Part 14: (Vol 11 no 5) rustproofing.

THE CAR
XJ S 3.6 Coupe manufactured 1988,
VIN: SAJJNAEC3CA15441,
purchased as damaged write-off December 1997.
Objective: repair, restore, run and upgrade.

XJ-S visits the Barber Institute of Fine Arts, Birmingham which was founded in 1932.

So, the finale is here. These 15 episodes have been pretty hectic. We've plucked a frontal damaged car from the salvage yard, straightened it out, rebuilt all suspension and brakes - and then suffered some typical problems experienced by XJ-S owners.

Of course, the project has gone way over budget (if there ever was fixed budget on a *Jaguar World* project car!) but then we never set out to do this on the cheap. Our goals were to prove that repairing a vehicle that has been involved in an accident is a well accepted and safe process, and the result can be every bit as good - possibly even better - as a similar car restored because of rust.

We also wanted to show the many and varied jobs that are needed on a typical XJ-S, from suspension rebuild to unleaded (or rather, low octane) fuel conversion. Along the way we did a cylinder head overhaul and tackled the conundrum of the fuel injection wiring harness. And this month we will show the fitting of an AJ6 Engineering large bore

throttle. The gain in performance should more than compensate for the slight loss due to the ignition retardation which is part of the unleaded conversion.

Probably the majority of cars on the road now have been involved in an accident or suffered body damage at some point. Only those beyond economic repair are 'written off'. It has nothing to do with safety, it's the accountants that rule here. Had our XJ-S been a late 4.0-litre convertible, the insurers would most certainly have taken a different view. It would have been repaired, returned to its owner and no more said. As it is, our 1988 coupe isn't worth that kind of money and so the assessor deemed it 'beyond economic repair'. The owner was compensated and the car sold on.

That a repair can be done economically using secondhand or aftermarket panels does not make the job any less valid. Think of it this way: what right has a 1988 car have to suddenly be given 1999 panels just because it has had a prang?

Our 1988 car now has 1990 panels. I'm okay with that. They're rust free and are now better protected than they ever would have been thanks to our rustproofing treatment. The few 'pattern' aftermarket panels we used came from David Manners and the quality of fit is really good. Coming from somebody who has just had an awful experience of poor quality reproduction panels (not all for Jaguars), that's praise indeed!

Breath of air
ROGER Bywater of AJ6 Engineering has this uncanny knack of being able to unleash hidden power (I wish he could do something for me!) and channelling it to good use. We had always intended to try at least one of his products on our XJ-S, but there came a point where we were actually forced into action. Back when we were suffering electrical glitches on the car, the air flow meter came up as faulty. We had the option of fitting another standard unit or grabbing the opportunity to try a large throttle body

Below: With the pipe loosened, the air flow meter can be lifted out of the engine bay.

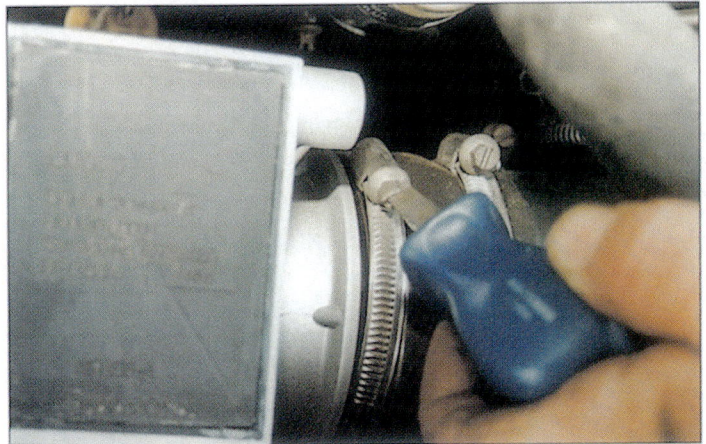

ype as produced by AJ6 Engineering. No contest.

Removing and refitting was elementary. The air flow meter sits between the intake trunking. Swapping over involved unclipping the harness (taking note of the earth wire), loosening the hose clips and removing the air filter housing. The meter could then be lifted out. Fitting the new meter was a simple reversal of the removal technique. It was interesting to compare the two side by side to see the bore of the enlarged AJ6 unit. Not just enlarged but flowed too, calculated for maximum efficiency.

On the road, the immediate difference was in the throaty sound of bigger intake breaths. This translated into performance as the accelerator called for response. I found that this XJ-S now has brisker than normal acceleration with better than average pick up. That it has been converted to run on regular unleaded fuel by using Jaguar's modified ignition pick-up made the results even more impressive. Fuel consumption remains as good as ever, my worse recorded figure being a shade over 21 mpg.

Where there's a wheel

LATTICE alloys are a very attractive style but they are an absolute nightmare to keep clean and brake dust soon discolours the outer face. I used Comma Alloy Wheel Clean and was impressed with the way it worked. But it was still a pain. As the existing wheels would need attention anyway, I jumped at a set of starfish alloys seen on the stall of XJ-S Spares at Spares Day. Fully reconditioned, they were a fraction of the cost of new. All that was needed now was a set of tyres.

Above: A multi-pin connector is unclipped in one go to take care of all the wiring. An additional, earth, connection is secured to one of the housing bolts though.

Right: See the difference in bore size between standard (left) and the AJ6 enlarged and flowed air flow meter. Modification is done on an exchange basis.

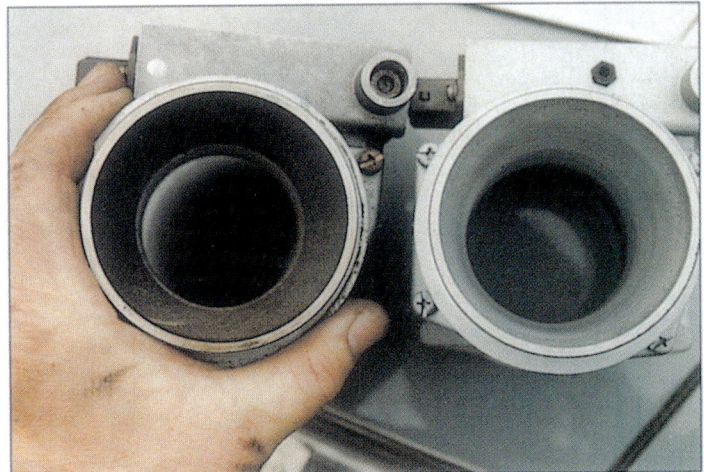

This is where I fell down on the job.

I had been ill. A sickness that had nothing whatsoever to do with a convivial Saturday with Alf Oloffson and Paul Wellington, playing with Enfield motorbikes and then an evening over a couple of decent bottles of France's finest. It went downhill from Sunday afternoon and did not improve until late that week. Groggy, I looked with glazed eyes in the workshop manual for tyre size, called Richard Jenkins Tyres and ordered five 215/70 x 15 tyres.

By the time they arrived I was feeling better and then realised my error. As from 1987, the XJ-S used 235/60 x 15 as Jaguar sought to make the car handle more crisply. Richard accepted my woeful tale and agreed to send out the correct spec while also collecting the first set. Richard Jenkins specialise in Jaguar tyres and can usually help with applications as diverse as Mk1/2, E-type, right up to current models. Pricing is very competitive too.

We had our (correct set) fitted by my local branch of Universal Tyres. I'm a pain in the neck to the lads there but they don't seem to complain. Enfield motorbike tyres one week, XJ-S the next. Nothing like variety though.

Conclusions

The XJ-S has been my only car. I've used it each and every day it's been mobile. It stood in the car park at Stanstead, it takes me out to cover features and forms part of my social life. So, what do I think of it? Well, here goes, with lashings of honesty.

The XJ-S is not my most favourite Jaguar. I've never owned one by choice, certainly not using my own money. This is by no means a general criticism, it's a very personal one. I like my sports cars to be in the E-type mould. Any bigger and I feel that the car is in saloon car territory and I'd prefer an X300 XJR (or even better, the XJR 'eight').

Original lattice wheels responded well to a good clean but are too fiddly for JP.

We found Comma Interior Clean worked well on the XJ-S's seats.

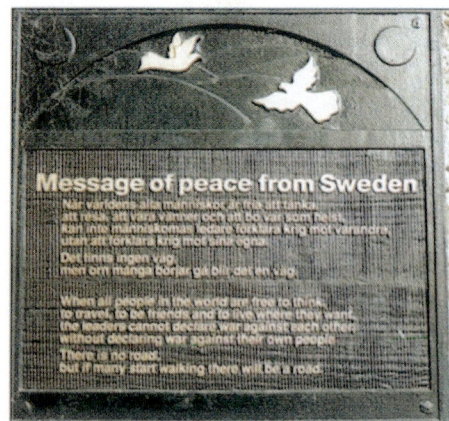

Fully refurbished five spoke starfish alloys bought at Spares Day will be a worthy replacement to the lattice type.

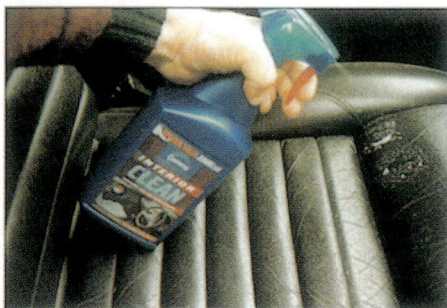

Message of peace from Sweden

Peace Square in Birmingham. In Sweden, the destination of the *Jaguar World* tour, they say: "When all people in the world are free to think, to travel, to be friends and to live where they want, the leaders cannot declare war against each other without declaring war against their own people. There is no road. But if many start walking, there will be a road."

I think that's where my problem is. I just do not care to own a grand tourer and that goes for Aston Martin DBs, Ferrari 400i or anything similar. The rest of team disagree and are all XJ-S devotees; perhaps that's why I was given the XJ-S, to win me over. And to be fair, to some extent it did.

On a cold and frosty November weekend, my wife Karen and I took the XJ-S for an extended weekend around Birmingham for the Motorbike show. The weather was grey and so was my mood. But this is where the strength of the XJ-S showed through. A selection of my favourite tapes and warmth from the heating system soon thawed my gloom. I felt comfortable in my cosy cabin. All round visibility was surprisingly good, despite the shape of the car. The motorway was crowded and so we took the back roads. In these slippery conditions the XJ-S did not fail. Late as ever, we put on a spirited charge and the response was magnificent.

Now I could see the worth of the newly rebuilt suspension, the wisdom of new brake discs. Handling was everything an XJ-S should be. Remember that by the time the 3.6 XJ-S reached this point in its life cycle, it came equipped with Sportspack suspension. I didn't even miss a manual gearbox (although I would have preferred this option) as the ZF

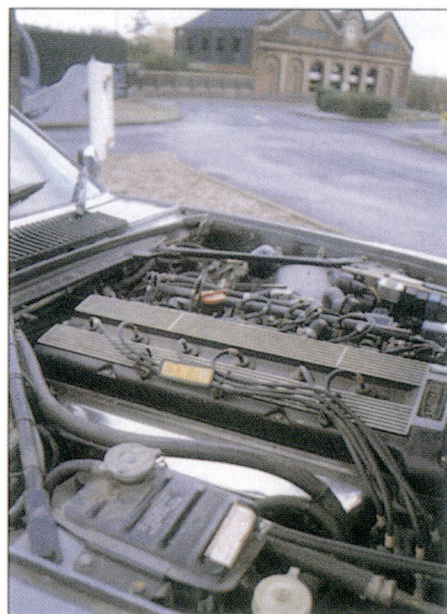

The 3.6 AJ6 engine gives a good turn of speed while returning respectable mpg figures. Seen here at the Black Country museum.

automatic shifter did a superb job, better in many ways, than today's offering (slightly less refined perhaps but at least the gears are there when you want them). By the time we booked into our hotel we just had time to dash out to find an accommodating Bistro.

For the next few days we played tourist. Art galleries, museums and excellent restaurants compensated for the extreme cold and grizzly weather. Our last day was at the Bike Show. We dreamt away on the Ducatti stand and loved the new Triumph. But our real money went on leathers and luggage.

Fully loaded, the XJ-S drove straight into the sort of traffic jam the British do so well. But we didn't care. We chatted, listened to music and mused over a few days well spent. Back home, the on-board computer told me that we had averaged 24.7mpg for the trip. Considering the type of conditions and the varying use we put the car to, I was impressed.

So, would I have another? Oddly enough, I think I would. But it would have to be on my terms. Ultimately, a 4.0 litre convertible with manual transmission could well be a persuading factor. I could give serious consideration to a 3.6 manual cabriolet too. Then a Lynx Eventer has always appealed. It's style and practicality would fit nicely into my way of life - I'm always carting camera bags and car parts about.

So there you are, I'm not so anti-XJ-S as would first seem. But time to move on. We'll soon see if living with an older Jaguar saloon is just a rose tinted image or absolute hell as my 3.4 saloon nears completion.

Acknowledgements

Large bore air flow meter from: AJ6 Engineering. Tel: 01625 573556. Tyres supplied by: Richard Jenkins Tyres. Tel: 01656 646498/657424. Fax: 01656 647743. Tyres fitted by: Universal Tyres. Tel: 01376 513213. Our thanks as well to all those concerned with the XJ-S project including David Manners (parts), Derek Swinger (paint), EH Autos (electrical/mechanical repairs), XJ-S Spares (used parts).

Part 2: Fettling

The Jaguar Monthly V12 XJS Lynx Performer which has just completed a schedule of fettling.

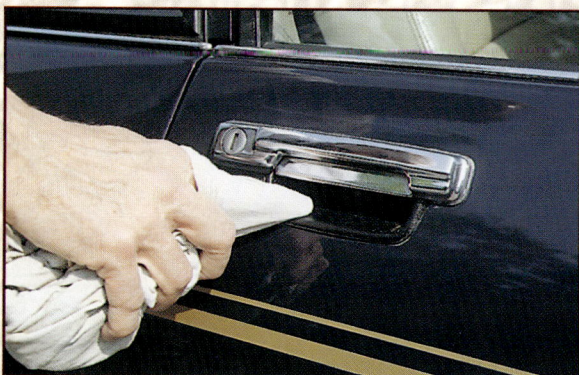

Door handle recesses are one of the first areas to rust and are very unsightly. Repainting is not too difficult. Regular applications of polish afterwards can help to prevent them rusting through again.

& Fettling

In many cases it doesn't cost a lot or involve much more than a little patient effort to bring about big improvements to a hard-used XJS. Martin Hodder and Gordon Wright explain how to add value to your new purchase.

Last month we covered buying an XJS – this month we tackle the 'fettling', a term we are using to cover the many small things that can be done to bring an XJS up to scratch. We are definitely not talking about engine or gearbox rebuilds or re-sprays, but jobs within the scope and capability of almost any Jaguar owner.

The XJS, with its refined, sleek and purposeful lines, responds more than most to tender loving care. Not only does it make it look its best, but a well cared for XJS somehow feels so much better when you drive it, and will command a much higher price when you finally get around to selling it.

To make the point we are looking at two cars; one a 1977 XJS, owned by Kate Parker of Gt Bardfield, which shows very little evidence of its 21 years; the other, *Jaguar Monthly*'s own 1986 V12, which underwent conversion into a Lynx Performer in 1990 and has just been through the fettling process in preparation for duty on the *Entente Cordiale*.

Get fettling on the exterior

The best place to start has to be with washing the car, the guaranteed way to learn all the intimate defects. For on-going care in this department the ideal scenario would be a wash every week (being sure to remove all the flies!), with a good polish once a month to steadily build up a protective layer on the car's paintwork (never polish in direct sunshine or when the bodywork is hot).

It is also at this stage (before polishing) that those unsightly stone chips can be tackled, with the dextrous use of a *little* touch up paint. The XJS still has plenty of chromework which needs a regular shine too, but can often be accomplished effectively with the bodywork polish (depending on the quality of the product used).

Avoid car washes – they simply don't seem to suit XJSs.

If the paintwork is looking particularly tired it might pay dividends to cut it back with a product such as T-Cut (used sparingly) before applying polish. In terms of

Plastic trim on the XJS can let the car down considerably when it fades or goes milky. Treating it is an easy matter.

If you never tried Armor All Tyrefoam you'll be surprised at the difference it can make.

cost this demands very little but in terms of effort it can be a major undertaking if done properly. If you have metallic paintwork you will need a special 'softer' cutting agent.

The XJS can commonly suffer from rust in the door handle recesses. This can be cured by the DIY amateur by rubbing down carefully, applying a rust inhibitor, a primer and two top coats of black paint (with rubbing down between each coat). It may sound a lot of effort but it is a very small area to work on and the difference it makes is surprising.

The XJS also has some plastic trim; a strip along the bottom of the front grille, and two pieces behind the rear side windows. The tendency is for these to fade to grey or go 'milky' in places. To restore them to a good black shine is very rewarding and can done with several proprietary products, such as Armor-All Protectant, Scrubs Inside & Out, etc. For the worst cases, mask the surrounding area and spray with can of black Vinylcote; again, a job that requires a bit more effort but pays off handsomely.

The wheels and tyres are an essential part of the fettling process and an XJS seen in profile will never look good unless these have been sorted. There are now many good products to take care of alloy wheels, and judicious use of a stiff brush will help to ensure a thorough cleaning. For the tyres the most outstanding product is Armor All Tyrefoam – spray it on and in about five minutes the tyres will have a superb natural (not painted) new look. Not only that, but this product also helps to keep tyre walls supple and prevents them getting too dried out and cracked.

Another little tip here concerns the rubber seals along the bottom of the XJS windows, inside and out. If they have become discoloured, spray a very small amount of Tyrefoam on a cloth and apply. It can have the same effect on rubber seals as it has on rubber tyres.

Interior fettling

Start inside the car with a thorough session with the vacuum cleaner. Carpets will almost certainly need a good clean. Some can be removed, but others will have to be cleaned *in situ*.

The XJS footwells are by far the largest floor area of the car, and to protect the newly-cleaned carpets it is well worth having some rubber mats that will cover the whole area. They are not an expensive item and the matting

Continued fettling and care accounts for this 1977 XJS belying its age.

There's plenty of leather in these XJS interiors. All leather needs to be fed using a leather cream. It can perk up a tired interior no end.

Tackle any signs of mildew spots on headlining early – as a fungus it will spread and take hold if not dealt with.

can be bought by the square foot and cut to fit, or you can have them made or buy ready-mades that are on the market. It is then a simple matter to remove them for high days and holidays to reveal your clean carpets.

Leather interiors need feeding with hide food – recommended frequency is

once every six months. If your interior is already well-worn, feeding will bring about an improvement. If your interior is quite bad with much wear and cracking then, as long as the leather is

Heavy-duty carpet cleaner is necessary for well-used car interiors.

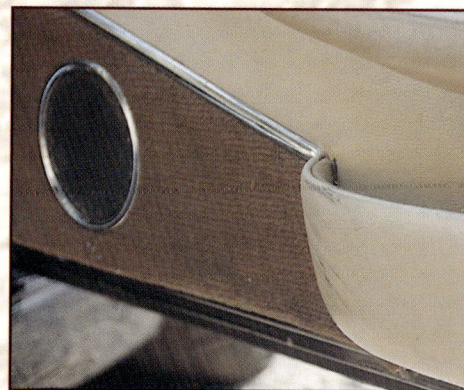
The forward end of the XJS door pocket is prone to scuffing. Use of a matching Vinylcote spray can is a good cure (make sure that the surrounding area is masked off first).

sprayed on here can hide the marks. The same applies to marks and wear that accumulate on the driver's seat side (usually the most ravaged part of the XJS interior)

Unfortunately, XJSs are notorious for damp in the boot and for water ingress from the scuttle (via the windscreen seals). In a car that has been kept outside for any period in wet weather, mildew can start to accumulate on the headlining. This can be cleaned off easily if tackled early; not so easily but still manageable if tackled later (in this

Try using an injector cleaner for better running results.

case take care because headlining can easily become detached).

A vast area of black vinyl above and around the dashboard tends to gather dust. This whole area can be given facelift with a simple application of Armor-All Protectorant.

Fettling the mechanicals

Jaguar engines last extremely well, but if yours is past its first flush of youth you can give a little helping hand by using an oil additive such as STP. Products such as this don't cost much, and when added at the same time as oil changes can make a difference in terms of prolonged engine life, quieter running, better oil pressure and reduced smoking.

If the engine is running 'lumpily', or surging while waiting at traffic lights, it could well be time for cleaning the injectors. An alternative might be to add Redex injector treatment to your petrol and run the your XJS on the motorway to the highest revs you dare (without getting a speeding ticket) for about two miles. This will help to remove deposits from the injectors, a process that can prove particularly beneficial to older cars like we ones we are featuring here.

'Antifreeze' or coolant does a lot more these days than simply preventing the engine's water from freezing solid. It protects the engine's cooling channels from corrosion, extends the life of the water pump and thermostat quite considerably, and reduces the likelihood of coolant boiling in extreme conditions. If you can, test for the correct percentage of coolant, and if in doubt, drain the whole system and start again!

Under-bonnet appearance can make a big difference to other people's

not cracked right through anywhere, it is worth getting the seats out and applying Vinylcote. This has to be applied with care, in several light 'mist' coats only – any attempt to cover with one heavy coat will meet with disaster.

Another tip; when using Vinylcote on seats that are starting to crack, first spray some of the product into the can lid, give it a few minutes to thicken a little and then apply right into the cracks with a small brush. This will disguise the cracks immediately – normal spray applications can never get into the cracks properly.

The door pockets on the XJS are very vulnerable and the driver's side invariably gets kicked and scuffed. If it is very bad, a little matching Vinylcote

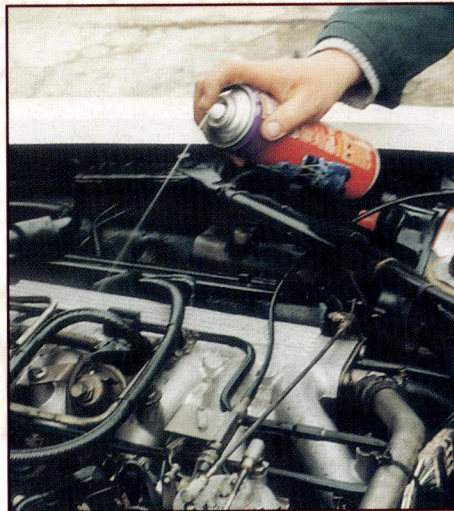

Spray engine degreaser around the engine bay and brush in well, especially to heavily grimed areas...

...then wash off, after protecting vulnerable electrical parts. The result should be a transformation like this!

Keep the rear valance rust-free and well-painted to enhance the XJS's appearance and prolong its life.

Cleaning rust from the discs of a car which has not been used for while can reduce wear to discs and pads.

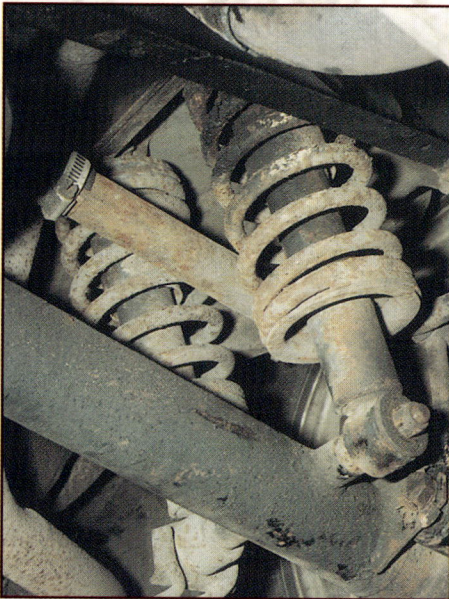
With the wheels off it's a good time to inspect the rear springs for broken coils...

...and the shock absorbers for leaks. This is a front unit.

perception of your Jaguar, especially to a potential buyer later on. Run the engine to get it warm, then apply a specialist cleaning spray all round the engine itself, the ancillaries, the inner wings, and everywhere else you can find grime. First make sure that you are parked on concrete or a surface which cannot be damaged by the products being used. Engine cleaners can make a dreadful mess of tarmac!

Leave the cleaner for a while to do its work (read the instructions) and then wash off. You could be amazed at the difference. To further enhance the appearance, spray afterwards with Duck Oil or a product such as WD40 for a gleaming engine bay.

On a newly-acquired Jaguar XJS, it pays to remove the wheels one by one to check the condition of the brake discs and pads (or get your local service engineer to do it for you). Look for scoring on the discs and be sure that the pads have plenty of wear in them, especially if you drive hard and fast. If the car hasn't been used for a while, you will find the discs have a film of rust on them. If this is the case, clean off the discs with some medium wet-and-dry paper. This will avoid harsh wear to the pads and discs that might

The finishing touch. Replacing number plates is not expensive and can make a great improvement. The old plate seen here was discolouring around the screw holes and the lamination was beginning to lift.

otherwise result when the car is first used.

While the wheels are off, take a look at the springs (there are two at each side at the rear) and examine the shock absorbers. You should look for breakages in the spring coils and any signs of leaking from the shocks.

Results

By the time you have finished this schedule of fettling you should have a car that will have been greatly improved on its original purchase condition and already improving in value.

It's then simply a matter of carrying on as you have started! ●

Thanks to...
• Mrs Kate Parker for the loan of her very fine 1977 XJS.
• Geoff Browne of The Garage, Gt Bardfield, Nr Braintree, Essex (01371 810909) for his very willing assistance.
• Halfords, for supplying a superb selection of car care products for use in this feature. The products were:
Car Plan Engine 'NV' engine degreaser
STP Oil Treatment
Redex Petrol Injector Treatment
Halfords Showroom Polish
T-Cut Metallic Colour Restorer
Turtle Wax High Gloss Car Wax
Halfords Interior Trim Treatment
Halfords Heavy Duty Carpet Cleaner
Halfords Upholstery Cleaner
Car Plan Triplewax Car Shampoo
Halfords Exterior Trim Treatment
Halfords Glass Cleaner
Halfords Colour Restorer
Halfords Touch-Up Paint
Halfords Traffic Film Remover
Halfords Colour Polish.
All these, and a full range of car care products and accessories, are available from local Halfords branches.
We also used Vinylcote, Armor-All Tyre Foam and Armor-All Protectorant.

XJS 3·6
SERVICE

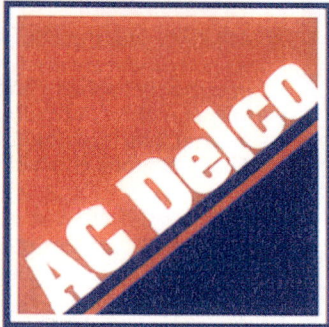
Jim Patten reckons that servicing the biggest of the big cats is nothing to be frightened of.

1996 is the XJS's last year in production – its replacement, the X300 will be here this autumn. The XJS body design has always been a bit contentious but its popularity cannot be denied. Many mourned the outgoing 'E' type but it's all too easy to forget that the XJS has been in production for almost twice as long with numbers made far exceeding the 'E' type.

Initially fitted with the superb 5.3-litre V12 engine (later modified to improve efficiency) the XJS gained a smaller six-cylinder engine in 1986. Not the classic XK unit as fitted to the saloons but a totally new design designated AJ6. Since its introduction this has proved to be extremely reliable and efficient with few inherent problems.

In general, an XJS should give years of trouble-free service but only if it's looked after. Neglect one at your peril. Unusual for such a modern car, there are still a number of grease nipples that need a visit from the grease gun. Worn suspension rubbers or sub-frame mounts can really upset the handling to such an extent that you will not even want to take the car out of the garage. However, if your XJS is set up properly, you really won't want to stop driving it.

Colin Armstrong had owned his 1990 3.6 automatic for about a year. He bought the car from a local main dealer and it came complete with a Jaguar extended warranty. Colin was thankful for this when a piston broke – a new engine was fitted under the warranty.

Because he's a fitter at Rainham Road Car Care you'd expect Colin to carry out his own maintenance. He also has use of the firm's facilities outside business hours. I joined him one evening as he embarked on a 15,000-mile service.

1. The AJ6 engine is usually pretty oil tight but always look for potential leaks and check all pipes and hoses. Replace any that you've the slightest doubt about – these are expensive engines to seize!

2. Remove the drain plug and drain oil into a suitable container. Never reuse the old washer – they always leak a little at least! Remember, you need to take the plug out to renew washer but, by then, the engine is full of clean oil.

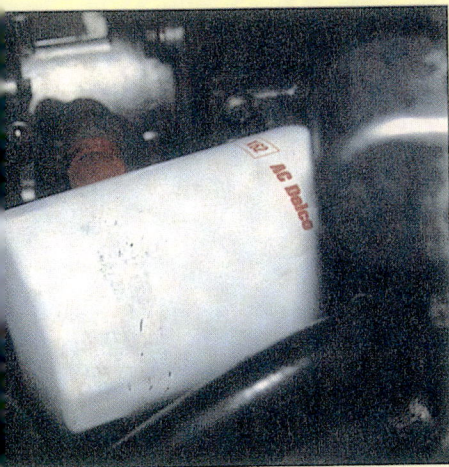

3. The oil filter is fairly accessible and gave readily after using an oil filter wrench. All old oil was cleaned away and a little grease smeared on the new filter's rubber seal before refitting using firm hand pressure only.

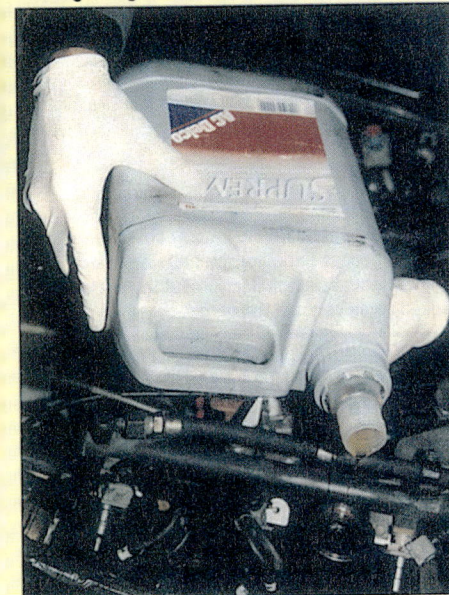

4. New oil is added (eight litres including filter). Start the engine and check for leaks. On these engines oil always takes some time to return to the sump so the dipstick won't show the correct level for some time. If it's on the knurled section of the dipstick, all is well.

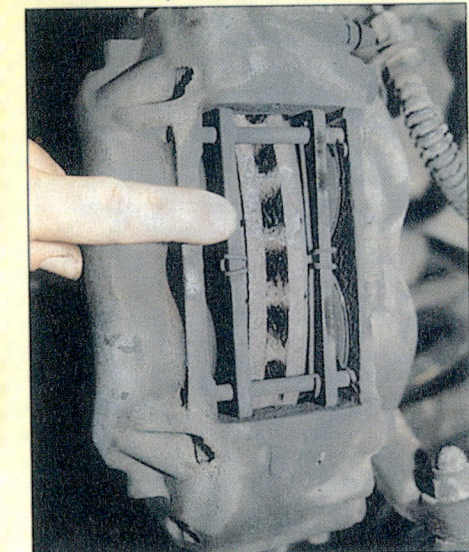

5. Like so many performance cars, XJSs can be heavy on disc pads, so check carefully. These are running a little low and will need changing soon. Discs are of the ventilated type which means they can't be skimmed if worn. Examine flexible brake hoses too.

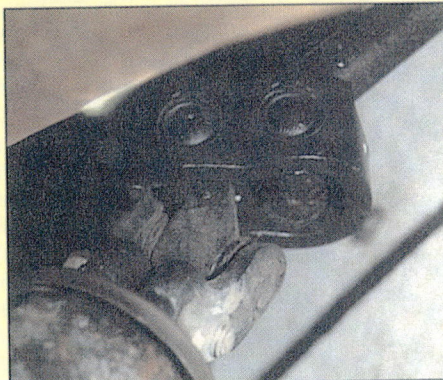

6. These universal joints on the steering column can develop wear or, if the car's standing, they can even seize up. In either case, the steering action and movement aren't helped.

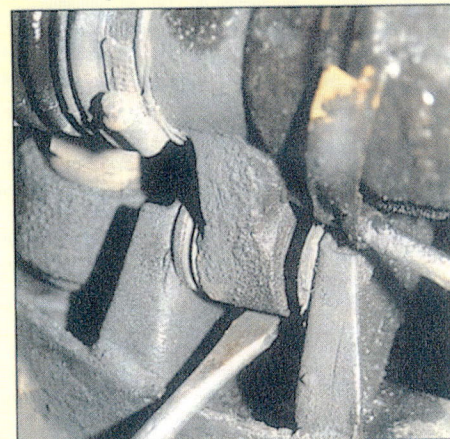

7. Steering rack mounts can fail due to oil attacking the rubber, giving steering a vague feel. Lever against the subframe (with large screwdriver) to check for movement. Replacement can be a bit fiddly. Check rack gaiters for splits/leaks with the steering on full lock.

8. With those big tyres a hefty load is transmitted to the wishbone bushes. Once it starts wear will be quick. A little rubber protection oil squirted around the join may help keep out the elements and put off a little the time when they all need changing.

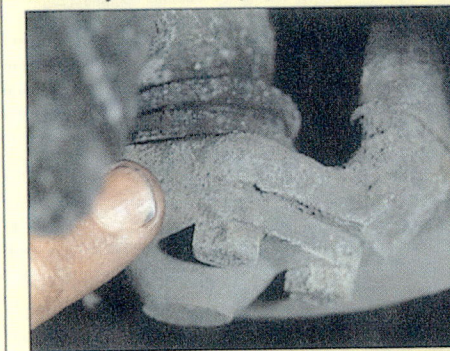

9. Earlier models used shimmed bottom ball-joints but, with the advent of the XJ40, sealed joints became standard. These new-type joints can be retro-fitted to older Jaguars – back as far as the Mk2 if you want! Each replacement joint is one fewer grease nipple to worry about!

10. Tapered needle roller bearings are fitted to the front hub. Occasionally these may need to be adjusted or re-packed with grease. As you'd expect, though, you can adjust them only so far before the bearings need replacing.

11. Check propshaft universal joints for wear and the bolts for tightness. Some joints have a grease nipple but this one is sealed for life. Check for wear by grasping each end and twisting in opposite directions. A joint with a lot of rust around the exterior may have seized – there's the reason for that drivetrain vibration!

12. The rear axle is located by radius arms. The rubber bushes at each end have a tendency to wear. When this happens the handling becomes very vague. The metal surrounding the arm mounting is very vulnerable to rust as well so inspect the whole area closely and carefully.

13. Four Metalastik mounts hold the subframe in place. To check them lift car so the subframe hangs on its own weight. A faulty mount will then separate from the rubber. Problems here make an XJS 'steer from the rear'. It's best to change all four – even if only one has gone.

...ugs, engine and cabin filters. Fax: 01908 352207.

77

14. There are four grease nipples on the inner lower fulcrum shaft and all need to be greased. Replacement is awkward, expensive and completely avoidable – if they're greased regularly these pins should last a very long time.

15. There's an access bung in the protective shrouds on the two drive shafts. With the bung removed, the grease nipples can be reached and greased. There are four universal joints in all – don't forget to do them all!

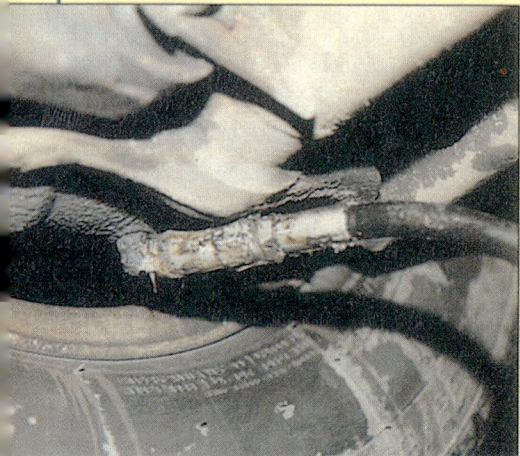

16. More grease points, this time the outer rear lower fulcrum shaft. See how the old grease is being forced past the outer seals. Don't neglect this lubrication – replacing the pre-loaded bearings is an awful job. Note the cable on the hub; this is for the ABS sensor.

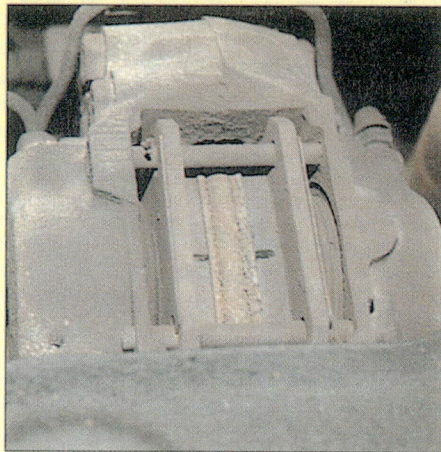

17. Plenty of life left in the rear brake pads and the handbrake pads above (not visible here). Just as well as changing them isn't pleasant. Jaguar handbrakes have a poor reputation but this is due to neglect rather than any overall design weakness.

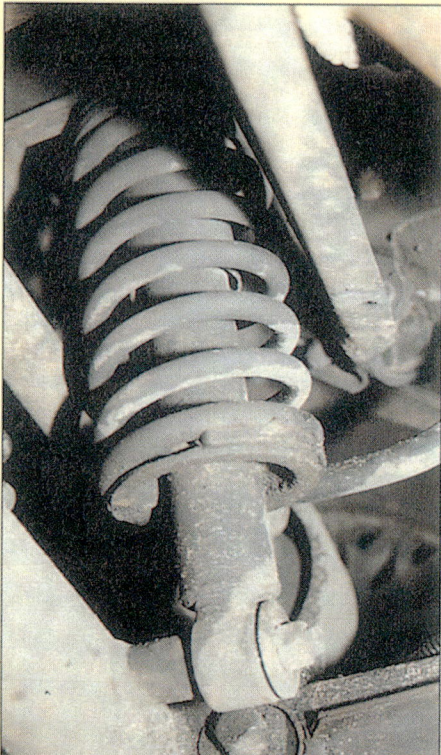

18. There are four shock absorbers at the rear and two at the front. Look for oil leaks around the shrouds and check the rubber bushes. Shock absorbers should always be replaced in axle sets. With the car on the ground do the 'bounce' test and expect it to return once only.

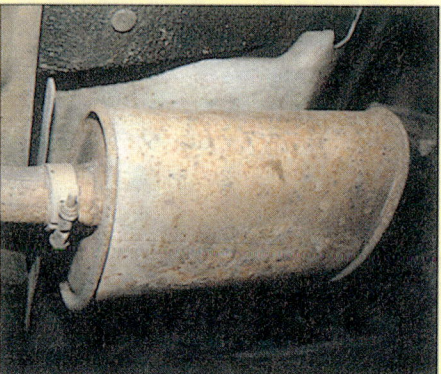

19. Jaguar exhausts are pretty long-lived, just as well because they're expensive. Check out all of the mounting points. If the pipe over the rear drive shafts sags, it can be damaged by the drive shafts. Replacing that pipe alone is almost impossible. Check fuel and brake pipe runs too.

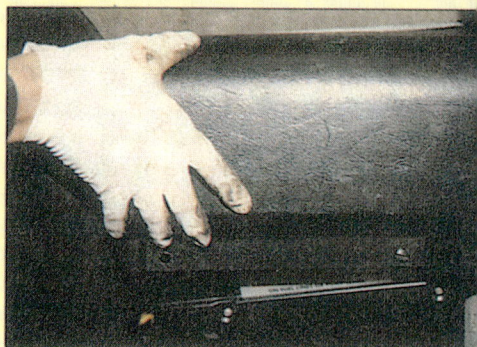

20. Battery lives in the boot beneath this plastic cover. Access is gained by turning the two retaining clips. Grease the terminals and top up the battery if it's not sealed for life. Battery should have a vent pipe to ensure any fumes exit from outside the boot.

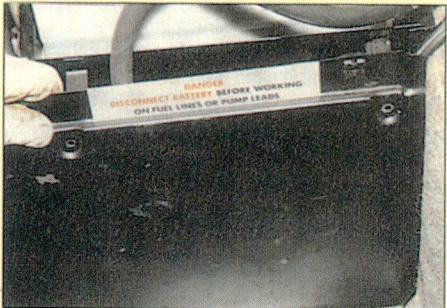

21. Just beneath the battery cover there's an access panel for the fuel filter. Two screws secure the top section but the bottom is tucked away beneath the carpet.

15,000-MILE SERVICE SCHEDULE

Engine:
- Renew engine oil & filter (every 7,500 miles)
- Renew air cleaner
- Renew spark plugs

Check levels of:
- Cooling system ● Transmission
- Brake fluid ● Screen washer
- Power steering
- Battery (if applicable)

Inspect or adjust:
- Check exhaust system
- Check brake pads & discs
- Check front & rear dampers
- Check coolant hoses
- Check steering rack gaiters
- Check prop-shaft & drive shaft joints
- Check steering joints
- Check tyres & pressures (including spare)
- Check drive belts
- Check all lights & indicators
- Check ignition timing
- Check CO level
- Check windscreen wipers & washers

Use grease gun on:
- Rear driveshafts
- Inner ower fulcrum shafts
- Outer lower fulcrum shaft
- Bottom front ball-joint (if applicable)
- Check horn ● Check seat belts

Lubricate all hinges, catches and accelerator linkages.

DELCO FREEDOM – The Truly Mainte

22. The spare wheel also has to come out to change the fuel filter. A clip secures each pipe with the bracket held by two bolts. Always make sure that the battery is disconnected before exposing any fuel lines.

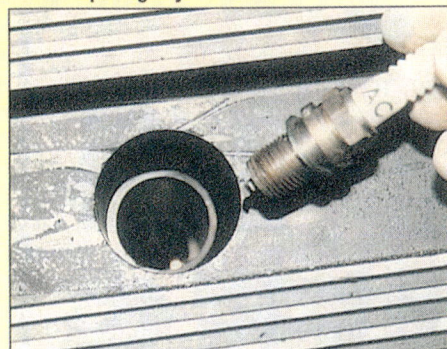

23. Spark plugs are recessed in the cylinder head so any oil leaks will soon fill the hole – so remove oil before undoing the plugs. When replacing the plugs, put some graphite grease around the threads so they come out easier next time. Set gap to 0.33 – 0.38in.

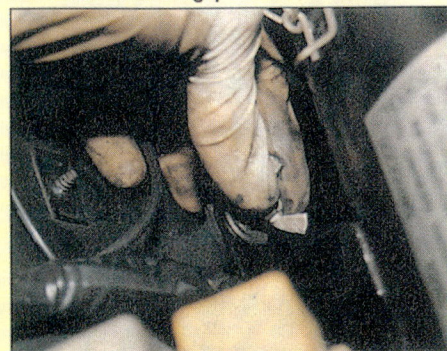

24. To change air filter element, loosen bottom wing nut on the housing bracket. Remove the top one completely and the housing is then ready to lift up. Unclip each end to free it from the pipework and lift away.

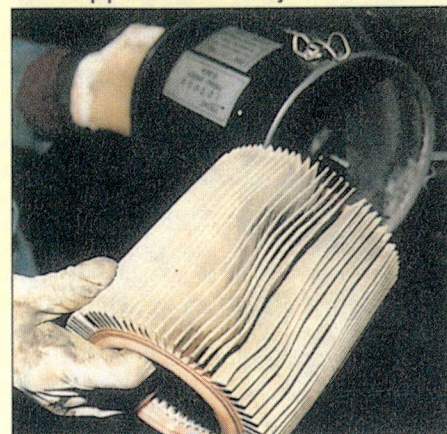

25. A nut holds the air filter in place inside the housing. Before fitting the new element, thoroughly clean the inside of the housing. When replacing, the housing is slid down under the washer on the lower wing nut.

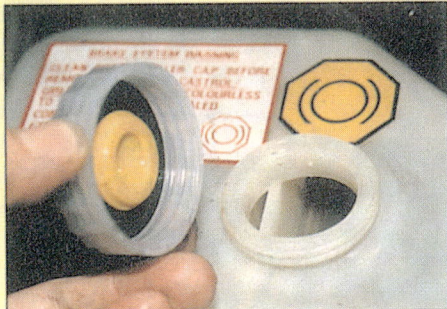

26. Check the level of the brake fluid; don't just rely on the dash warning light. It is extremely important to change the fluid every two years anyway. This is an unpleasant job on Jaguars due to the inboard rear brakes and it's therefore often overlooked.

27. Check power steering fluid level; the level indicator is fixed to the cap. Just to confuse things, the cap twists off clockwise – not the usual anti-clockwise! Use power steering fluid if a top-up is needed.

28. An hydrometer is used here to check the anti-freeze. If you have any doubts over the existing mixture, then replenish the system using at least a 33% mix. Check the levels of coolant and screen wash.

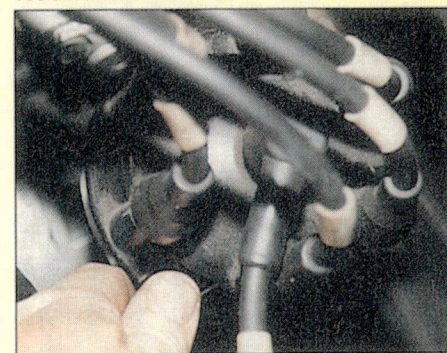

29. Although there are no distributor points with the fully electronic ignition system, it still pays to check the distributor cap and the rest of the system for condition. Poor HT leads will lose a lot of power – replace them if in doubt.

HEALTH AND SAFETY

Servicing your car at home is perfectly safe as long as you're sensible. There are, however, a few points to watch.

● Take care over jacking and supporting. Never work underneath a car that's supported only by a jack – use proper axle stands under a sound, secure part of the underframe.

● Never attempt to raise or support on car on sloping, uneven or soft ground. And always chock the wheels at the end not being raised.

● Take care when cleaning out brakes not to breathe in asbestos dust from worn pads and/or linings. The tiny amount of dust produced by one car won't harm you but, if you're servicing brakes regularly, wear a face mask as the cumulative effect could cause problems long-term.

● Oil is hazardous. Any that gets on to your skin should be washed off immediately and applying some barrier cream first is strongly recommended.

● Always dispose of old oil thoughtfully – pouring it down the drain is illegal and damages the environment. Most local authority dumps have a facility for collecting old oil as do some garages.

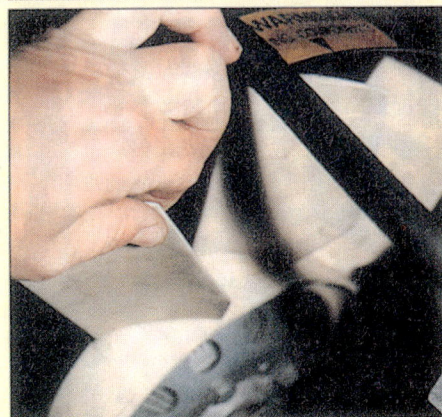

30. The viscous cooling fan should have slight resistance when spun. Rocking it back and forwards also checks out the bearings. Beware if it's gone – replacements are very expensive. It is still a surprise that electric fans were not used.

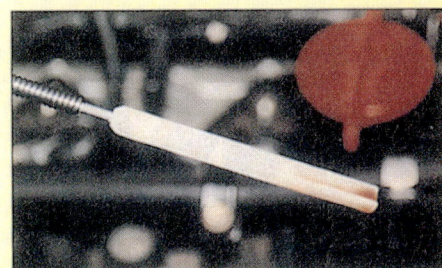

31. Checking automatic gearbox level. Make sure the car is level and with the engine running select 'P'. With the footbrake applied, move the selector through each position before returning to 'P'. Leave the engine running and check the level on the dipstick. Note the colour too – a brownish hue means it needs changing. A slightly burning smell is a sign of internal problems.

Apart from the front brake pads, this XJS needs no extra work. The rear axle oil was checked through the combined level/filler plug but so restricted is the space that we were unable to photograph it. The engine breather filter was checked as were all lights, horns and indicators and the accelerator linkage and door/bonnet catches greased. There's a fair selection of drivebelts on these engines, all of which have to be examined for condition and have their tension checked.

Our thanks to Rainham Road Car Care (Tel: 0181 592 3887) for allowing us access after dark.

CLEAN ENGINE BREATHER

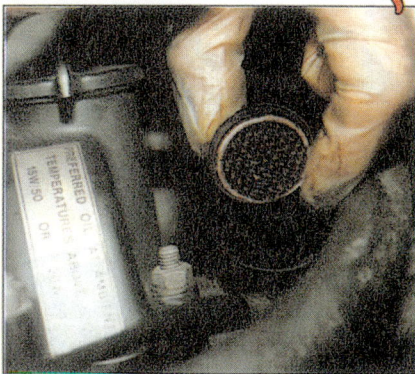

Engine breather is situated to the front left-hand cylinder head. An 'O' clip secures the rubber elbow. Remove the elbow and extract the gauze filter. This can be washed out in petrol and then dried. Ideally use a new 'O' clip when replacing the elbow.

TOP UP POWER STEERING FLUID

Unscrew the power steering cap and look at the built-in dipstick. Top up if necessary using automatic transmission fluid. If the steering squeaks a bit, a power steering additive often helps eliminate the noise.

LUBRICATE ACCELERATOR LINKAGE

There are an awful lot of throttle links under the bonnet and all need lubricating, an area often overlooked. While the can is out, apply a drop to all catches and locks.

CHECK/CHANGE AIR FILTER

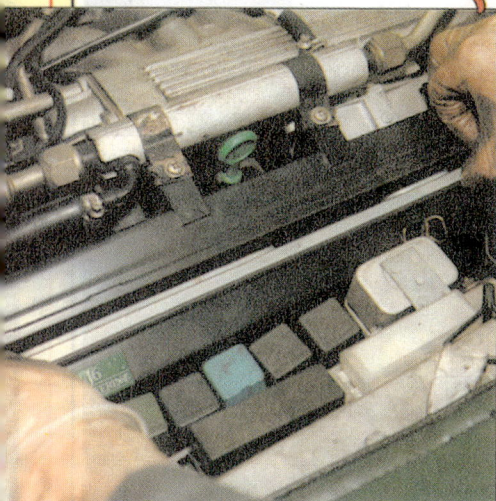

This job is pretty straightforward but clearance between air filter housing and inner wing is a bit limited. Access is gained by releasing the spring clips. Jaguar recommend that the seals be changed as well. Remember there are two air filters.

CHANGE FUEL FILTER

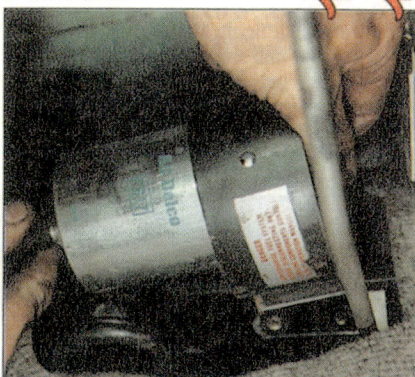

It's into the boot area for the fuel filter. Jaguar recommend that the system be depressurised first – do this by disconnecting the cable from terminal 85 on the fuel pump relay and pulling the HT lead from the ignition coil. Then crank engine a few times to depressurise the system. Unclip inlet and outlet hoses and attach to new filter. Don't forget to replace the disconnected wires. Battery also lives in boot – it's unlikely to be a top-up type so all you have to do is check the connections.

UNDER THE FRONT

CHECK BRAKE PADS AND DISCS

The brakes on any Jaguar work very hard. Martin not only checks the pads and discs visually, he attaches a dial gauge to the disc to check bearing end-float (should be 0.05-0.15mm) and for disc distortion. XJS discs aren't as expensive as you'd think.

CHECK STEERING RACK BUSHES

Those who don't know better dismiss the old XJS as a bit woolly on the steering. That's because the steering rack mounts have worn. Grab a stout lever and see how much play there is. If they need renewing, Classic Spares market sports bushes that really sharpen the car up. They also offer a tool that saves having to remove the whole rack.

CHECKING STEERING JOINTS AND GAITERS

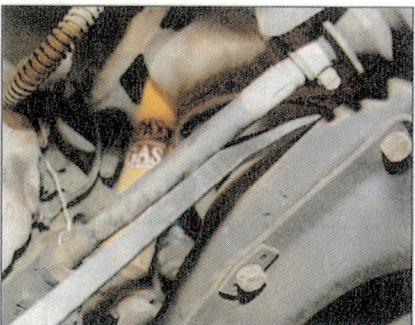

With the trusty lever still in hand, push against track rod, checking for play in the steering rack and track rod ends. If the rack has worn then an exchange unit will be needed. Check gaiters for cracks too. You'll know if it's torn as fluid will pour out. If the gaiters are cracked, replace immediately.

FRONT BALL JOINTS

Later models are fitted with sealed for life ball-joints. However, earlier cars have joints that are shimmed and need greasing. This actually dates back to the late forties. If the old type of joint wears, change it for the modern type – it's a direct replacement.

UNDER THE CAR (REAR)

CHECK/TOP UP REAR AXLE OIL

Filler/level plug is in the most inaccessible place at the back of the rear suspension unit. The plug is ½in and can therefore be reached with a socket universal joint. Top up if oil is below the level of the hole, and Jaguar recommend changing it every 12,000 miles. Use the correct power lock differential oil.

PUMP GREASE INTO GREASE NIPPLES

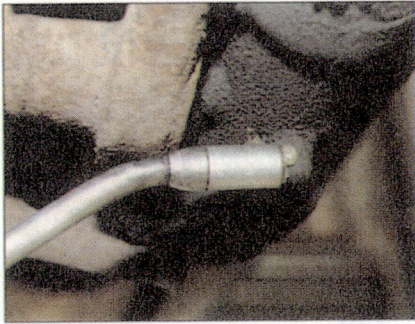

Almost uniquely, Jaguar retain grease nipples – one at the bottom of each hub, two on the inner lower wishbone fulcrum shaft and a grease access hole in the top of the hub. Additionally, each drive shaft has a nipple in each universal joint under a bung. Clean away old grease and dirt before applying new grease.

CHECK SECURITY OF BOLTS

Go around the car checking all nuts and bolts for security. Those needing special attention are on the propshaft and steering parts. Caliper and some other safety-critical bolts are sealed with lock-wire and will not need tightening – but check the wire's condition!

REPLENISH BRAKE FLUID (1)

Brake fluid should be renewed every eighteen months/18,000 miles. This operation has been done a few times on this car. Later XJS' have ABS brakes with an accumulator so brakes are not bled in the conventional way. With the engine running, constant pressure is applied to the brake pedal. Martin has a special spring loaded tool for this job. Jaguar recommend that all hydraulic seals be renewed every three years.

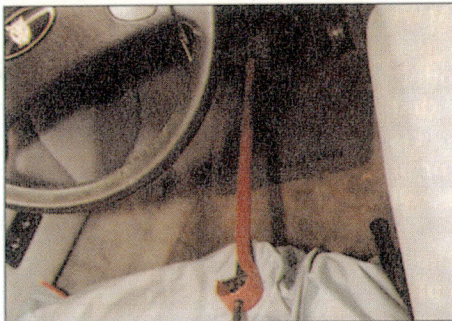

REPLENISH BRAKE FLUID (2)

Attach bleed tube to the caliper bleed nipples (inboard at the rear and tricky) and loosen nipple. Brake fluid will then flow through the tube. You must keep the reservoir constantly topped up. When new fluid flows through, close nipple. Jaguar recommend using special fluid to expel the old fluid first before re-filling with fresh.

BEYOND THE SCHEDULE

CHECK RADIUS ARM BUSHES

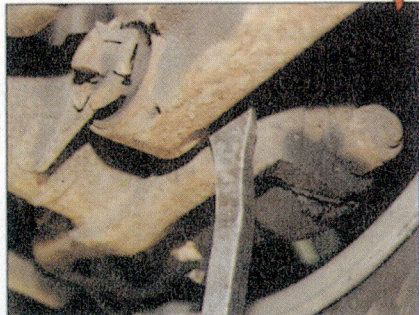

Apply a lever against the large and small radius arm bushes and check for wear. Also look for rust, especially around the radius arm mount. It is not unknown for the arm itself to rust. This one has surface rust showing and is due for some rust treatment.

CHECK FRONT SUBFRAME

After a while, the paint on the front subframe starts to peel off. This can actually lead to serious rusting and be potentially lethal. We have seen some quite late cars afflicted with this. The only solution is to replace the subframe. Better still, catch it early and treat it.

CONCLUSIONS

There is still more to do. Checking the automatic transmission fluid is routine. Engine running, go through the gears resting in Park. Check the level with the engine running. Fluid and filter should be changed every 24,000 miles. This involves removing the gearbox sump therefore worth all of 👎👎👎👎.

Check rear hub's endfloat. It should be between 0.026-0.076mm. Rear discs and pads should be examined too. Changing pads is within most people's capabilities, but the disc change is quite involved. Check all subframe mounts visually by supporting the car on a jack and allowing the frame to 'hang' on its mounts where the worn ones will quickly show up. Apply grease to handbrake cable at front and rear where the bare cable is exposed and runs through sliders.

Watch tyre wear too. If it is not truly square, then either an adjustment is out or there is wear present. As there are many adjustments available, seek advice from a specialist. Always apply Copper Ease to the rear of aluminium wheels and re-fit wheels to a torque of 55Nm.

Jaguar's XJS is certainly a more complicated device than most cars, but one well cared for is extremely rewarding. It would certainly be advisable to equip yourself with a Repair Operation Manual available from Classic Spares. While not a fully fledged workshop manual, it covers everything that most owners need.

Our thanks go to Ray Ingman at Classic Spares (01992 716236) and to Martin Pike of Classic Engineering, Jaguar repair specialist (01992 788967).

lugs, engine and cabin filters. Fax: 01908 352207.

83

The Jaguar X

Nigel Thorley looks at one of the rarest of the XJS models, definitely a 'sleeper', which he predicts will one day be amongst the most sought-after of all modern Jaguars.

From any angle the cabriolet looks good. This 3.6 litre model has the later lattice alloy wheels fitted.

The Jaguar XJS had come through some controversial times since its announcement back in September of 1975. At that time it was so very different to anything Jaguar had done before – a car that you either liked or disliked.

At one point production had to be temporarily stopped due to poor sales and then, in 1981, with the introduction of the 'HE' model and a much improved fuel efficient engine plus a change of trim style,

the fortunes of the XJS changed literally over night.

Changes thereafter came fast and furious but two significant announcements were made at the same time – October 12th 1983. First Jaguar announced the launch of a brand new six cylinder engine, the AJ6 3.6 litre multi-valve power unit. Destined eventually for a new saloon model, this engine, like the XK and V12 units before it, would first be seen in a sports car. So it was, with the new XJS 3.6.

Commanding a top speed of 145mph,

with a 0 to 60mph acceleration time of 7.6 seconds, the smaller engined XJS could also boast excellent fuel economy with over 25mpg easily being obtained. This was helped by the fitment of a new German Getrag five-speed manual gearbox which provided for long-legged cruising; in fact the XJS 3.6 in fifth gear at 70mph was only running at 2,464 rpm.

Enter the cabriolet

Although this engine was released in the XJS coupe, the second major step forward

JS Cabriolet

for Jaguar was to reintroduce a drophead model, the XJ-SC (XJS cabriolet).

Jaguar had long been criticised, particularly by the valued American market, for not producing a convertible model after the demise of the E-Type in 1975. At that time the company thought the age of the drophead had gone and followed suit with many other manufacturers at the time. However, the pressure for convertibles was so great that, after several outside specialists converted existing XJSs for individual customers, the company set to work on developing a new drophead based on the XJS.

The launch in October of 1983 was an exciting time for Jaguar and the marketing strategy was to emphasise this as a very special car. As well as being available with the new engine and gearbox the car received the same Starfish alloy wheels reserved with the V12 coupe, all leather upholstery (including door panels) and a revised rear accommodation area without seating.

No new bodyshell

In order to get the cabriolet out as quickly as possible it was decided to use the same bodyshell (but suitably strengthened) and to go for a targa type top arrangement rather than re-engineer an entirely new shell to accept a conventional convertible layout. Therefore, the XJ-SC model bodyshell was built alongside conventional coupe models in Castle Bromwich. At this stage the roof was left off, as was the back panel forward of the boot lid. The bodyshells were then shipped to Park Street Metal Company, who removed the remaining buttresses from the rear wings and welded in new tops and a revised panel to the rear of the boot lid.

From there the bodyshell came back to Birmingham for painting and then went off to the Browns Lane assembly lines for mechanical and trim fitting, but still without the roof finished.

Jaguar had negotiated a deal with Aston Martin in Milton Keynes for their Tickford body division to finish off the trimming on

Around 60 cars left the factory with fitted rear seats at the special request of buyers, but this was never recommended nor officially recognised. Nowadays, many other cabriolets are being converted, which is quite an easy job to do using conventional XJS seating and trim.

the cabriolet models. They made and trimmed the two fabric-covered targa tops, the rear hood material and mechanism and any detail trimming required to the inside.

After the Tickford 'treatment' the cars went back to Jaguar for final finishing and check-over before despatch to the dealerships.

To give structural strength, both the cant

rails and new targa centre bar incorporated tubular steel. These were located at the 'A' posts, rear wings and extended to the lower sills. Strength beneath the car was provided by transmission tunnel stiffening and a rear cruciform cross-member (under the rear suspension).

Correspondingly, although the door frames and windows remained unchanged,

Internally, XJS cabriolets are no different to other XJSs. Note that this particular car is equipped with the half leather, half tweed upholstery.

1 The 'procedure' for removing the top is quite lengthy. With the tops in place and hood erect, at a distance the cabriolet looks little different to a conventional XJS convertible.

2 Each targa panel can be removed independently, held in position by two clips released from a central chromed handle. The underside of tops and the hood are fully trimmed.

3 Just like having a sunroof open (the car can be driven with one or both targa panels removed). But, with the rear hood still erect, speeds above 50 mph do create a degree of buffeting as the air gets trapped inside the back of the car. Better to leave the targa panels in place with the hood folded down.

new rear quarter-windows and surround were fitted. The re-location of the fuel tank filler had to be accomodated (by this stage with saloon-type filler and lock), and, of course, so did the new rear compartment area.

Why a two-seater?

Since the car lacked a conventional roof, Jaguar were concerned (later proved to be unfounded) about the degree of strength in the bodyshell, and this was one reason why the cars were not fitted with rear seating as standard.

Allied to this were concerns that, in the event of an accident, anyone sitting in a rear seat could be lifted and thrown forward to be decapitated on the targa cross-bar. This

was a concern that remained, no matter how unlikely it was.

So, a carpeted luggage area was fitted in the cabriolet models with chromed support bar, occasional pockets in the front and two lockable cubby-holes for storage of valuables. A very neat and practical arrangement.

The versatility of the hood and targa top arrangement provided excellent opportunities for the occupants to enjoy various degrees of open air motoring and Jaguar even made available a fitted hard top for the rear compartment for the winter months (at extra cost).

Cabriolets came on the market for the 1984 model year at £20,756, a £1,500 premium over the 3.6 litre engined coupe

and £1,000 cheaper than the V12 coupe. Jaguar made the claim that cabriolets would only be built to customer orders, but this didn't turn out to be the case.

On the crest of a wave

By this time XJSs were selling better than ever and so it was decided in July of 1985 to expand the cabriolet theme with the introduction of a V12 engined version which allowed Jaguar access to the American market with this model. Sales were initially very good although many Americans complained about the 'awkwardness' of man-handling targa roof panels and manually lowering the hood when they were so used to electrically-driven hoods from a button on the dashboard!

4 *To release the hood, a single catch in the centre unclips it from the centre and at both sides allowing the hood frame to be folded flat.*

5 *With the hood down, the tonneau cover is clipped over and...*

6 *...hey presto: you have a convertible! With the support top bar not being obtrusive and the side frames still in position, it means you can enjoy open top motoring at most speeds without undue buffeting.*

With modifications to the V12-engined XJS coupe the 12-cylinder cabriolet was also updated to match, whilst the 3.6 litre model continued unchanged until February of 1987 when, for the first time on the smaller engined model, automatic transmission was made available (a four-speed installation).

This was accompanied by other somewhat cosmetic changes to the cabriolet with new sports seats, veneered centre console area, the use of walnut instead of elm woodwork, stainless steel sill tread plates, new steering wheel and the option of the new-style lattice alloy wheels.

In September of 1987 the deletion of the cabriolet models was brought about by the forthcoming launch of a new and 'proper'

full convertible version of the XJS. The total production of XJ-SCs only amounted to just over 5,000, making the car quite rare by modern Jaguar standards. The rarest, of course, is the 3.6 litre with automatic transmission – merely on the basis that it was the last model introduced.

Production figures

3.6 litre manual transmission	963
3.6 litre automatic transmission	183
5.3 litre automatic transmission	3,863
Total made:	5,009

Cabriolets today

Owning a cabriolet has its advantages and disadvantages and we take the latter first, then we can set the scene for enjoyment.

First, although Jaguar enjoyed better sales and a significant improvement in quality control during the period that the cabriolet was in production, in real terms the car was still a triumph over adversity. The cars still had rust problems, those dreadful bar instruments on the dashboard, poor switchgear and all the other usual complaints you get with the older XJSs.

Second, there is that targa top that takes time to remove and replace. Then you have to store the targa panels in the boot, taking up valuable space – so a cabriolet is not necessarily the ideal car for a long touring holiday. The cars produced up to 1986 particularly are prone to leaking from the roof area. This was a common problem that only seems to have been cured when Jaguar

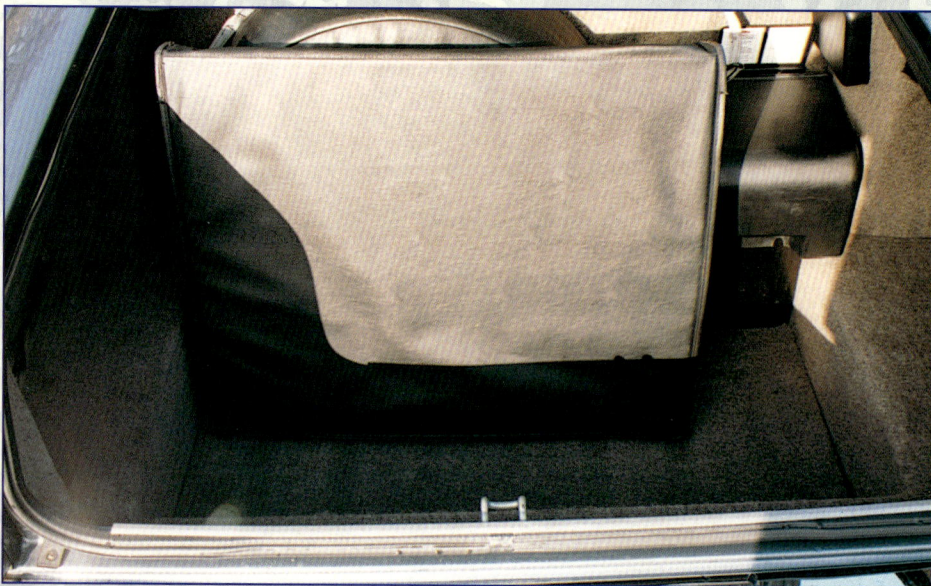

No boot space is lost to the cabriolet until you come to store the targa panels. An upholstered envelope is provided which does take up some room. It is possible to put in and remove the targa panels when you have luggage in the boot – but it takes some practice! When buying a cabriolet, check that the boot lid is not dented from the inside out. This happens because the targa panels are not square – so, if you put them in the wrong way and shut the boot lid...

The rear compartment treatment on cabriolets is different to other XJSs, but a similar treatment was later adopted for the convertibles as well. Plenty of space to store extra luggage lost from the boot area...

took the final assembly back in-house late that year.

Vision can also be a problem with the top up or down. With the hood in place vision through the rear quarters is bad and the hood has a conventional perspex panel that tends to go opaque after a while. With the hood down it rests on the rear deck, so restricting an important rear view area.

So what is good about them?

First, and, most importantly at the moment, they are CHEAP! Yes they are slightly dearer than an equivalent XJS coupe but still significantly cheaper than the early 1987/8 convertibles (which were only available with the V12 engine anyway). They're currently the cheapest way to get into rag-top Jaguar motoring (check out our price guide in last month's issue of *Jaguar Monthly*).

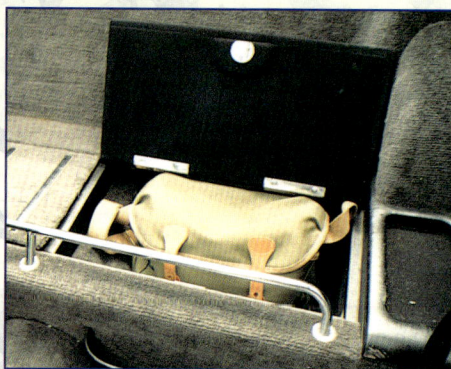

...and lockable boxes are very useful to store items like cameras.

The targa top arrangement makes for a very rigid structure, again much more so than the XJS convertibles and, from the comfort side, with the hood down and the targa panels removed, you do not get the

usual buffeting associated with convertibles. You can drive very pleasantly at motorway speeds with only a little wind in your hair and can listen to the radio at normal volumes.

Rarity must also come into the equation. With so few produced they are not a common sight on our roads and therefore must rate as a good buy and investment for the future.

Which model?

Although so few were made it is amazing how many you see for sale (particularly during the winter months). It does seem that many owners get the 'bug' for rag-top motoring, and then progress from a cabriolet to a fully-fledged convertible (although they may not always be happy with the change once it is made!).

Cabriolets are no different to other XJSs in the way they deteriorate, and it must be born in mind that these were bought as regular everyday cars, so they will have suffered the ravages of time and road salt like any other model. The best advice is to buy the best you can afford regardless of colour scheme and specification.

If you are nit-picking, then the very late cars with the revised seating and walnut woodwork look the best (and the seats are more comfortable). Conversely, late 1986 onwards cars (made totally in-house at Jaguar) seem to be of a slightly better trim quality than the earlier cars.

Most items were standard equipment on cabriolets like air conditioning, stereo equipment, alloys and leather trim. However, many cars have an on-board computer and some have half leather, half tweed upholstery which is warmer to the 'bum' than all leather (particularly when you leave the roof down).

For the best economy and most practical use then a 3.6 litre engined model is best. Although the automatics are very rare, they don't perform as well as the manual version, which allows the opportunity to take advantage of the engine's willingness to rev freely and give you the best acceleration performance. V12s are the smoothest by far, but petrol costs and maintenance make them less practical than the sixes.

Conclusions

If you are looking for a great buy, the cheapest rag-top Jaguar in the land still with a full parts bin availability, many specialists at cheaper than dealer prices, rarity and classic car insurance rates, then the XJ-SC is the car for you.

Get one quickly, they are disappearing fast!

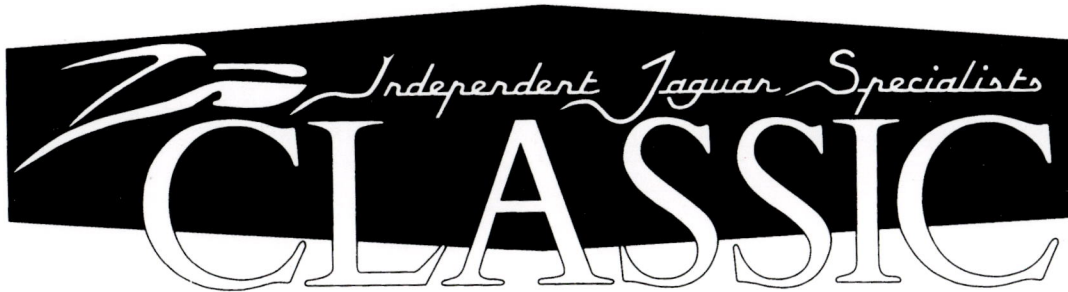

Jaguar XJS 4.0-litre convertible

This month we take a look at the car that everyone thought would be overshadowed by the XK8... but wasn't!

The XJS has been an incredible model for Jaguar. With a total production run of over 115,000 cars spread over 21 years, there aren't those many models from any manufacturer that have survived for that length of time and are so well respected today.

Background

Surprisingly, when the XJS was announced in 1975, it did turn heads but for the wrong reasons. As the most expensive production model from Jaguar at the time it's 'modernistic' styling approach certainly wasn't to everyone's liking and it took several years to establish itself.

The advent of the HE V12 engine helped to make the car more economical and appealing, but it wasn't until 1983 and the launch of the six-cylinder models that the interest in the XJS grew and all the models benefited from improved build quality and reputation.

Particularly in the North American market, there was a need for another Jaguar convertible and the half-way-house cabriolet never quite fitted the bill. It took an outside organisation in the US to develop such a car, details of which were later adopted by Jaguar themselves to form the true XJS convertible available for 1988, although at this time only the V12-engined model was available.

It wasn't until 1992, one year after the XJS restyle, that a 4.0-litre

six-cylinder version of the convertible came along, which was one factor in the continuing success of the model range.

The 4.0-litre XJS convertible remained in production until the very end of the XJS extended life and the last cars received the Celebration treatment, effectively making them a special limited edition.

Model history – first cars

The 4.0-litre XJS convertible was announced in the summer of 1992. Not only was it the first time you could buy a true Jaguar XJS convertible with the smaller six-cylinder engine, but it was also the first Jaguar to be fitted with a driver's airbag, albeit at the time as an extra cost option for £700.

The price when new was £39,900, listed initially at that price with the

The original 4.0-litre XJS convertible when released in 1992 had conventional styling with traditional rubber-faced bumpers, although this car does feature the new styling features from 1991.

The later, post-1993 4.0-litre convertible, now with the AJ16 engine. Note the revised bumper bar treatment.

All the 4.0-litre convertibles benefited from the uplift styling at the rear. This later model features the square tailpipes from the 1994-onwards models.

£45,450. This effectively made the 4.0-litre convertible a very prestigious and somewhat 'select' motor car which, even at this price, found many keen buyers – buyers who normally would have steered clear of the massive V12-engined version.

Better models

June 1993 saw the next development of the 4.0-litre convertible when the whole range was upgraded to enhance the customer appeal. Externally the cars were recognised by their new moulded bumper bars matched to the body paint colour. At the front the bumper incorporated the spoiler.

At the rear new square tailpipes were used and the model also benefited from new 7in x 16in five-spoke alloy wheels.

The interior of the convertible now offered for, the first time, 2+2 accommodation with specially-made occasional seats in the rear compartment, even if they were a little cramped for anyone over the age of seven.

For this change the bodyshell and floorpan had been totally redesigned,

five-speed Getrag manual gearbox.

Optional extras included the four-speed ZF 4HP 24 automatic transmission for £1,370, forged lattice alloy wheels at £1,010, heated front seats with memory settings for £960, full leather upholstery (half leather standard) for £510, cruise control at £490, fog lamps £150, power headlamp wash £360 and, of course, that air bag.

So, although the XJS convertible was well equipped, if you went for the full 'pack' it would have set you back the not inconsiderable sum of

All 4.0-litre convertibles had the analogue instrumentation. This very late Celebration model also sports the wood/leather steering wheel and contrast piping to the seating.

Manual transmission 4.0-litre convertibles are more common than most people think and despite 'stick shift' cars being generally worth less than autos, for today's enthusiast buyer of an XJS this shouldn't make a lot of difference.

Production Numbers

1993	4.0-litre convertible	3,803
1994	4.0-litre convertible	2,309
1995	Moulded bumpers/AJ16 engine	2,324
1995-1996	(including Celebration models)	5,490
	Total production:	**13,926**

What one could call the 'mid-term' 4.0-litre convertible. At this point (1994) it features colour-coded light surrounds and wing mirrors and the blackened grille.

Later frontal treatment. Although the XJS finally retained the blackened grille, it got back the chrome light surrounds and wing mirrors.

The rear seating was always a bit of a joke but it can be useful for the very young.

To accommodate the rear seating, the bodyshell had to be structurally altered to allow the hood to retract below seat level.

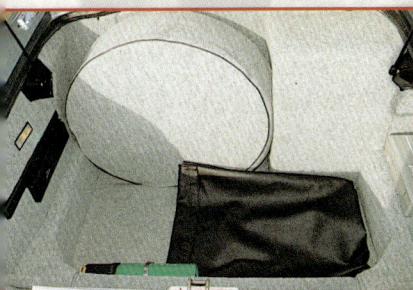

The later 4.0-litre convertibles lost some boot space because the hydraulic ram pump had to be moved somewhere. To the left is the Jaguar-fitted CD player which, although an extra cost option, tended to be fitted to most late model cars.

which also meant changes to the hood and its mechanism.

With the hood hydraulic ram pump now re-sited to the boot area and the rear window made a little shallower to enable the hood to still fold away to below rear seat level, the only other change was aesthetic in making the hood tonneau cover in Ambla (instead of cloth) and matching to the upholstery colour scheme.

New sun visors with illumination, improved air conditioning system, warning 'chimes' to show doors open and seat belts not in use, plus an integrated alarm system, all improved the overall standard of trim in the 'new' cars. Standard equipment now included the driver's air bag, ABS, catalytic exhaust system, limited-slip differential, cruise control, automatic transmission and power-operated seats.

While the coupe models at this time gained a new Sports pack suspension system, the convertibles remained with the softer 'Touring' version, although the extra anti-roll bar, Bilstein shock absorbers, etc. could be specified at extra cost and are worth seeking out today on an intended purchase.

A significant mechanical change came with the fitting of outboard rear disc brakes, making for ease of maintenance. Also by this time ZF steering racks were now fitted.

A lot of 4.0-litre XJSs came out with half leather upholstery.

Full leather only came in as standard equipment on the last of the cars when the seat pleating was also revised.

Prices had inevitably risen by this time with the 4.0-litre convertible coming in at £41,400 – but remember that it was much better value for money when you took into consideration the previously extra cost options.

The much improved AJ16 version of the 4.0-litre power unit came to the convertible in 1994. Providing 7% more power and with new pistons, engine management system and on-board diagnostic capability, this engine followed the developments for the X-300 saloons.

For the same year the new interior seat design with the 'ruched' style was used and on the exterior the 4.0-litre benefited from colour-coded grille and headlamp surrounds.

A Celebration

The final fling for the XJS 4.0-litre convertible came in 1995 and 1996 when the last of the cars were made available under the Celebration name. These were effectively the

Hood down or up, the XJS convertible still looks the business.

same 4.0-litre cars as before, but now with a special range of metallic exterior paint finishes, diamond turned alloy wheels and a quality gold badge to the bonnet top.

Internally, the quality continued with embossed headrests, leather centre console lid and contrast seat piping. The veneer was of a finer quality sapwood walnut with a wooden gear lever knob and half leather/wood steering wheel of new design (taken from the later XJ40s).

By this time the price of the 4.0-litre Celebration convertible had risen to £45,950, but this model epitomised

Despite some fears that many dealers would inevitably be left with XJSs when the XK8 appeared, in fact virtually all the final XJSs were sold, such was still the demand for the XJS convertible at that time.

The demand for the model has remained strong since, to the point that very few 4.0-litre convertibles currently come onto the market and Jaguars dealers are always keen to get their hands on them.

It is surprising to note that these late-model XJS convertibles have not been hit by the XK8. They are a very different motor car and many feel that the XJS was certainly a unique Jaguar in style and appeal.

Current trends

Despite the fact that the most recent XJS

4.0-litre convertible is now getting on for three years of age, the prices are holding up remarkably well. Quality also seems to be well assured as the majority of cars on offer seem to have low mileages due to being used as second vehicles.

Even the early cars are worth considering and are significantly cheaper than the later upgraded models. All the 4.0-litre convertibles benefited from the extra strengthening to the bodyshell and so don't suffer from the same stress factors as the earlier V12-engined convertibles.

The XJS 4.0-litre convertible must be an excellent buy and good investment for the future. Compare the prices now with any comparable upmarket convertible and you will realise what good value for money they are. Also, if you think they will reduce much further in price, then watch this space; note that the earlier V12 cars have never seemed to drop below the £11/12,000 mark for the last couple of years. Remember that the numbers made are not great, so demand will always be reasonably high.

the final development and quality of the XJS.

As you can see from the production figures, the XJS 4.0-litre convertible was a modest success but was significantly boosted by the introduction of the later model upgrades and with the forthcoming demise of the model in favour of the XK8.

Leslie Thurston explores the surprisingly complex world of Jaguar badges, beginning in this issue with the XJ-S

Badges: a car's 'jewellery' – identification, adornment and, very often, the representation of an almost priceless asset in terms of brand name. Yet perhaps countless millions of car owners, if asked, probably could not accurately describe those on the very car they are driving.

Originally, nameplates on motor vehicles counted for little and were often not in evidence. Early bespoke vehicle manufacturing was a veritable cottage industry where corporate identity in any form was of little importance. However, the rapid development of parts standardisation and the assembly line highlighted the need both to distinguish one maker's product from another and to establish marque identity, in what was soon to become a ferociously competitive industry.

Initially, this was through simple name plates carried over from the former carriage making trade. But, within a short time, specially designed badges appeared, usually on the radiator, followed by an ever increasing array of mascots and other decorative features, some of which have endured to this very day in one form or another.

With many up and coming car makers centred around Birmingham and the Midlands, where better for them to have their badges made than the Jewellery Quarter in the very heart of Birmingham itself? Jewellery firms, some established centuries before, were ideally equipped to produce the beautiful enamelled badges which, up to the 1950s, few cars were without. But these chrome and enamel artefacts were very labour-intensive to make so, in the late 1940s, alternatives appeared in the form of injection moulded acrylic (plastic) badges. Nowadays, enamelled badges are a rarity, the majority of car manufacturers using cheap substitutes often lacking any degree of artistic merit.

Leslie Thurston has one of the world's largest collection of Jaguar badges and mascots.

Fortunately for Jaguar owners, 'our' company still insists on good quality products, upholding the image of one of the world's finest cars. This is certainly true of the XJ-S; the car this article is concerned with.

The last production 6.0-litre V12 XJS Coupé and 4.0-litre Convertible to roll off the Browns Lane assembly line simultaneously on 4 April 1996 were infinitely superior to the original September 1975 launch model. Even so, the first XJ-S was quite superb, despite being rather plain compared to the run-out Celebration Coupé and latter-day gorgeous convertibles.

Ask any classic XJ-S owner how many badges adorn his car and the answer is likely to be two, three, or possibly four, but not many more. He or she is almost certain to overlook one on each wheel, rear number plate and reverse light assembly badge, the often very attractive horn push and, last but not least, adhesive label badges on the engine cam covers. Look around any XJ-S long enough, and the leaping cat emblem, jaguar growler face or corporate name will become evident on all sorts of internal fitments, right down to key fobs and the keys themselves. Most of these do not merit inclusion in a general description of XJ-S badging but even the most insignificant have entailed some degree of design and planning within Jaguar.

This general description of XJ-S badging concerns standard factory production home market cars only. Special editions, export models and outside conversions will be the subject of further articles..

XJ-S COUPÉ 1975 – 1981

Grille – injection moulded acrylic tapered badge mounted at centre of black slatted chrome-surrounded intake Grille. Corporate Jaguar name in separate box at top with number 12 inside a large V in lower box. Gold on black background.

Boot – Chromed die-cast metallic separated XJ-S lettering at right side of black number plate panel. NOTE: These and the contemporary XJ6 Series 2 boot (trunk) lettering were the last chrome metallic script badges used on Jaguars.

Reverse Light Number Plate Lamp Assembly – Acrylic strip badge displaying large size corporate Jaguar name in black lettering on striped silver background, mounted between reversing light lenses.

Wheels – Acrylic circular disc badge showing gold Jaguar 'Growler' face on black background, mounted on chromed cap clipped into centre of wheel.

Horn Push – Injection-moulded elliptical badge displaying gold growler face, surrounded by gold tooth border against an attractive gold/bronze background.

Cam Covers – Adhesive label badges with Jaguar name in gold inside gold semi-elliptical frame with plain black background.

The use of gold symbols and lettering on this model identifies it as having a V12 engine. This followed the practice started with the introduction of 12-cylinder engines in the XJ Series of saloon cars. The gold growler Grille badge on

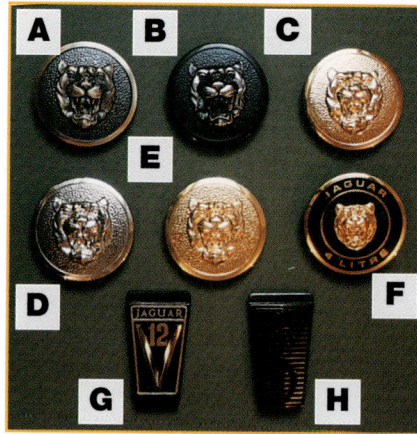

Bonnet and Grille badges: (a) First growler badge on 1981 H.E. model. (b) More common black version used to end of XJ-S production. Also used on XJ220s. (c) Gold plated growler fitted to some 6.0 litre models and various special additions. (d) Rare chrome growler only seen on special racetrack Pace Car XJ-Ss. (e) Later 6 litre gold chromed version. (f) Enamel 4 litre Celebration badge. (g) Acrylic V12 Grille centre badge 1975 to 1990 facelift. (h) Die-cast Grille centre badge, 3.6 litre models only.

the first 4.2 litre XJ6 is one exception to the rule, (there were a few others). Generally, six-cylinder Jaguar cars of this period had silver features on the main badges, mostly with a black background.

1977 saw minor modifications to external chrome work, the most important being the change to an all chrome grille. The former black rear number plate panel was now finished as body colour.

XJ-S H.E. 1981

To improve fuel economy, the May head engine was introduced in July 1985. Known as the XJ-S H.E, many changes to trim, brightwork and badging came too. The chrome die-cast XJ-S boot lettering gave way to larger injection moulded letters still situated to the right hand side of the number plate, and to the left, matching H.E. lettering identified the new model. Reading H.E. XJ-S from left to right caused slight confusion to some so later, the badges were transposed to read XJ-S H.E.

The plastic Jaguar plaque badge in the

reverse light/number plate lamp assembly now appeared as raised chrome lettering on a black background with much wider typeface, in keeping with that of contemporary Series 3 XJ Saloon boot script badging.

The most significant addition to XJ-S badging came in the form of the now-familiar die-cast bonnet growler. Up to now, the sleek bonnet had been devoid of chrome strips and other decorative features (the old style Jaguar leaping cat mascot had long since been abandoned by Jaguar in the interest of safety). Initially, the growler badge had a darkened bronzed finish with attractive two-tone burnished rim and prominent face details. This seems to have been a short lived variant as it was soon replaced by the more familiar blackened version.

October 1983 saw the next major XJ-S development: the 3.6-litre AJ6 engine in Coupé form and innovative (for Jaguar) Cabriolet. Several new badges appeared on these two models, starting with a very smart blackened polished die-cast badge mounted in the grille. As with the larger engined car, this retained the Jaguar name in the upper box, while a letter S occupied the lower space in place of the V12. This may have been directed at American buyers as the XJ-S is often referred to in the USA as the 'S' type. The horn push now had a silver growler face and matching toothed border against a black background identifying its six-cylinder engine.

In 3.6-litre Coupé form, the large XJ-S boot script badge to the left of the number plate remained as on the V12 with a new matching 3.6-badge to the right. With the Cabriolet, the XJ-S script badge became XJ-SC and a pair of small die-cast chrome leaper badges adorned the BC posts just above the door handles.

The front end of the new AJ6 engine cam cover carried the same adhesive Jaguar name plate as fitted to the V12 covers.

For the next two years the V12 Coupé still carried the title XJ-S H.E. with no change to badging, until the introduction of the V12 Cabriolet when the H.E. was dropped. A new V12 script boot badge replaced the H.E. lettering and now the

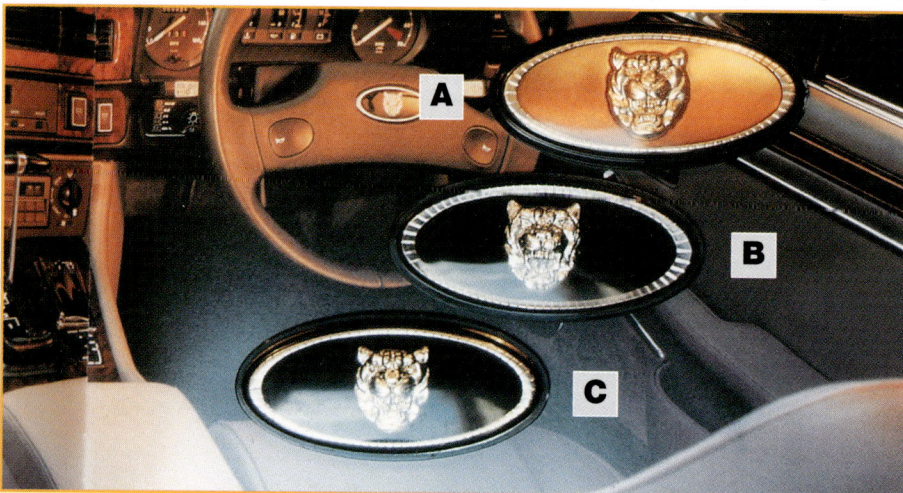

Horn push: (6) Original V12 horn push 1975-1988. (b) 3.6 litre silver and black version. (c) Gold and black version common on later models up to introduction of steering wheel airbags.

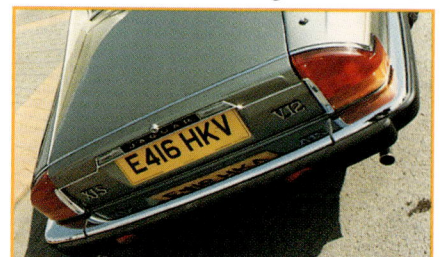

A 1987 model V12 Coupé; the H.E. badge has now been dropped.

V12s were badged XJ-S V12 or XJ-SC V12 depending on model.

The introduction of the beautiful XJ-S V12 convertible in April 1988 came without any significant new badging. The horn push background changed to black, which was about all.

May 1991 heralded a comprehensive facelift inside and out. While the bonnet growler remained, the grille badge was dropped altogether. A completely restyled rear end bootlid carried small sized JAGUAR XJS script badging on the new 4.0-litre engined Coupé and JAGUAR XJS V12 on the two larger models, the 'dash' between the letters having been dropped. At this time there was no 4.0-litre convertible.

The old style reverse and number plate lamp assembly had gone along with the classic stop and rear lamp units. The boot lid was now adorned with a full width heavy chrome finisher without nameplate or other decoration. Both 4.0-litre and V12 models shared the same gold and black horn push but there were changes to the matching coloured wheel centre badges. These were now held in chrome instead of plain black bezels. One noticeable difference to the wheel badges was a much enlarged growler face.

Under the bonnet, the new 4.0-litre engine cam cover adhesive badge changed to black lettering on a silver background. The new V12 engine sported a pair of impressive large metallic plate badges with chrome Jaguar V12 lettering and border on a black background.

A 4.0-litre convertible arrived for 1992 and, with it, a driver's side airbag became an option. This was in the steering wheel under a new style embossed cover; the beautiful classic horn push was soon to disappear forever.

In addition to increasing the V12 engine size to 6.0-litres in 1993, more cosmetic changes occurred, both internally and externally, including colour keyed bumpers. Some 6.0-litre XJSs came off the assembly line fitted with gold plated bonnet growler badges and also sported V12 boot script badges on the wings. Later, gold chrome was used on the growler as a more durable alternative.

Throughout Jaguar's long history, we have seen how new engines destined for future saloons first appeared in sports models. This occurred once again in June 1994 with the introduction of the forthcoming X300's AJ16 engine in the 4.0-litre Coupé and Convertible. Differing quite radically in appearance from its AJ6 predecessor, the new engine came with a neat, easy-clean cam cover, made even tidier by the addition of a smart injection moulded JAGUAR

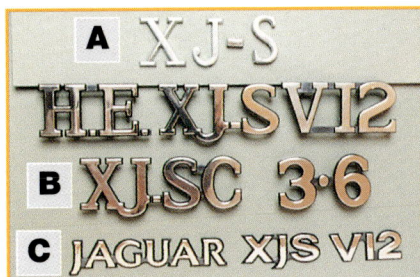

Rear boot lid badges: (a) Original die-cast lettering 1975-1981. (b) Large size injection moulded script badges from 1981-1990 facelift. (c) Small size injection moulded script, facelift models only to end of XJ-S production.

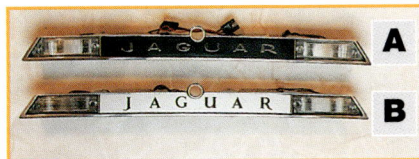

Reverse light number plate lamp assembly: (a) 1981-1990. (b) Original 1975-1981 version.

Wheel centre badges: The original wheel badge is shown centre, and the most widely used black bezel version in the bottom left hand corner. The remainder, with chrome bezels, were used at different times in later stages of production.

embossed sparking plug coils access cover. So the same cover could be used on other six-cylinder engines, the Jaguar name only appeared in raised lettering – the 4 LITRE was stencilled on afterwards.

One more significant XJS variant was to appear before this illustrious Jaguar

ceased production altogether. Knowing prospective buyers might prefer to wait for the forthcoming XK8, a tempting new XJS model, commemorating Jaguar's 60th anniversary, was announced in May 1995. Called the Celebration, both Coupé and Convertible versions must surely be the most superbly appointed of all standard factory XJS models. A very special car like this deserved rather special badging, which turned out to be amongst the most attractive seen on Jaguar cars for decades. Finished in gold and enamel, it was the first badge of its kind used by the company in 40 years. Mimicking earlier Mark 2 Grille badges, the central golden growler face was set in a green sunburst background, with the inscription JAGUAR 4 LITRE in the surrounding black border. Quality badges like this are extremely expensive and may never be seen on other standard Jaguar models again.

This description does not cover all minor changes to wheel badges which occurred during the final years of production, and has also omitted details of tread plates, some of which have separate adhesive JAGUAR nameplates. Other badges appeared on the centre consul for various reasons, sometimes to blank off unused switch apertures on models lacking certain refinements.

Attractive badges always give that special finishing touch to any car and an XJ-S would certainly appear much the poorer without them. Finally, almost certainly some XJ-S owners reading this will have badges which differ from those described. There are all sorts of reasons for this – incorrect badges are often fitted during repairs or restoration, while sometimes they are deliberately changed by owners desiring something different. It is also not unknown for cars coming off assembly lines to have non-spec badges when there are temporary shortages.

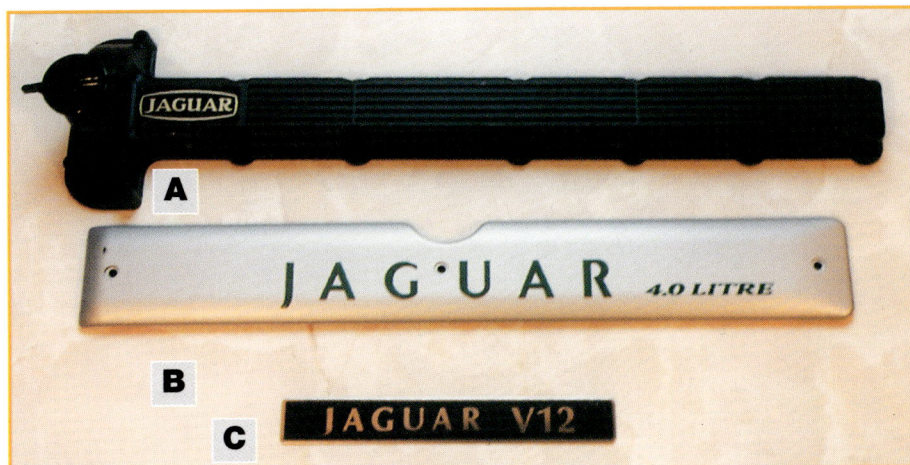

Cam cover and engine badges: (a) Typical V12 engine cam cover with adhesive JAGUAR name badge. (b) Late model 4.0 litre AJ16 engine spark plug coil cover plate. (c) Chrome and black metallic nameplate on facelift V12 revised inlet manifolds.

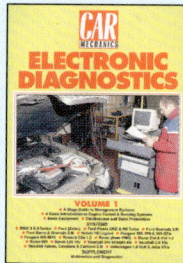

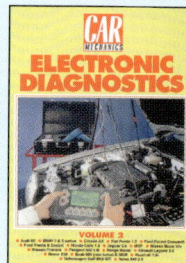

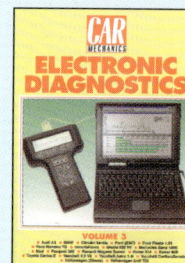

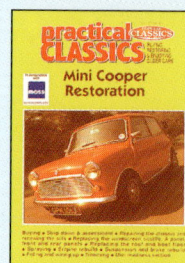

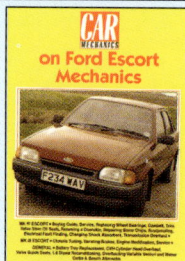

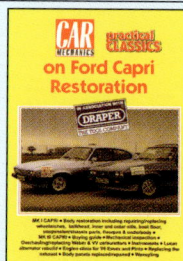

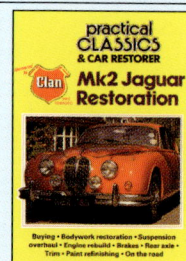

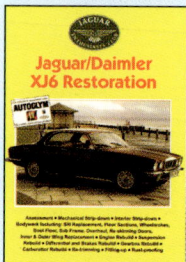

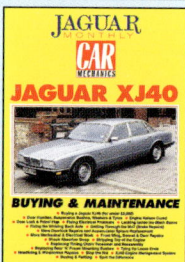

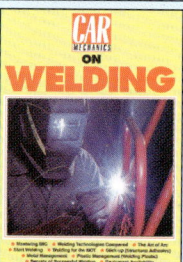

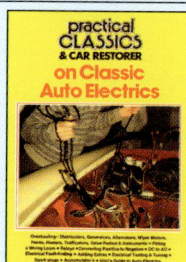

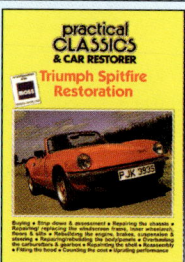

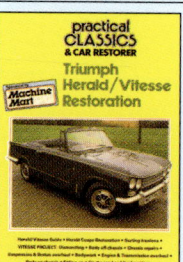

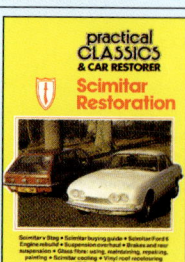

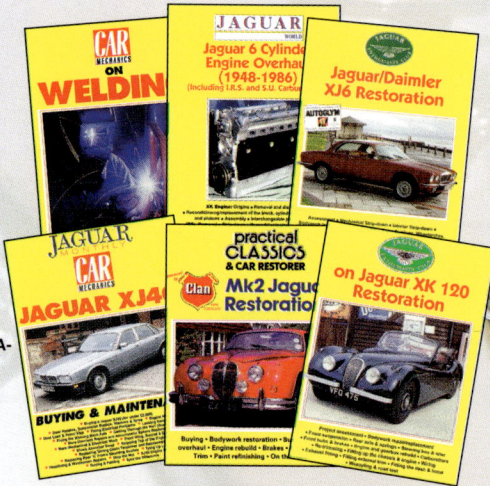

100